Cultural Interactions

For the Chilean people

Cultural Interactions

Conflict and Cooperation

Frans-Willem Korsten

Amsterdam University Press

Cover illustration: Edward Clydesdale Thomson

Cover design: Gijs Mathijs Ontwerpers, Amsterdam
Lay-out: Crius Group, Hulshout

ISBN   978 94 6372 038 0
e-ISBN   978 90 4855 617 5
DOI   10.5117/9789463720380
NUR   757

Table of Contents

Part 2   Cultural Selves

Acknowledgments

This book was conceived in the years 2016-2021 and written in the course of the years 2020-2021. It is a COVID-19 book in the sense that it is based on the podcasts that I started to make when all teaching had to go online for a second year BA course in the Leiden University Department of International Studies in The Hague. Podcasts cannot be too long, so there were two of them for each session. The very genre of podcasting provoked me to think of music, and the music in turn provoked me to think about why I would choose to relate a specific session, and its content, with this or that piece. The COVID-19 years certainly had their effects on content, but equally strongly provoked a host of questions on form(s). It is hard to say 'thank you' to the circumstances that formally changed the format of this book, but at least it needs to be acknowledged.

I was helped in writing this book by comments by or conversations with especially young colleagues working on similar issues, all with their own expertise. I am grateful to Gerlov van Engelenhoven (especially), Aida Gholami, Zeynep Gültekin, Andries Hiskes, Yasco Horsman, Bram Ieven, Looi van Kessel, Adam Marcus Patterson, Sara Polak, Miriam Retter, Renee Turner, and Tessa de Zeeuw. The Department of International Studies in The Hague was helpful and generous in giving me the chance and the time to develop this course, as well as by providing me with input into the process. Here, I want to thank Joost Augusteijn, Paula Esteves dos Santos Jordão, Jaap Kamphuis, and Tim de Zeeuw.

Then there is the more general intellectual climate where issues dealt with in this book would pass or be considered within a variety of meetings, where we were thinking and talking or, perhaps more importantly, I was listening. In this context I would like to thank the Leiden University Centre for the Arts in Society and its director, Sybille Lammes. Other colleagues who were of importance in making this book, in the present or the past, are Nuno Atalaia, Maria Boletsi, Thomas Bragdon, Cui Chen, Kai-wen Chiu, Maghiel van Crevel, Esther Edelmann, Kornee van der Haven, Gert Jan Hofstede, Isabel Hoving, Yasco Horsman, Nancy Jouwe, Çağlar Köseoğlu, Inger Leemans, Liesbeth Minnaard, Greta Olson, Sara Polak, Shailoh Philips, Aafje de Roest, Dorine Schellens, Mineke Schipper, Nanne Timmer, Berrie Vugts, Astrid van Weyenberg, and Kitty Zijlmans. I thank Oscar Man, Lucy McGourty, Margo de Koning and the AUP editor for their editing. Mistakes remain mine.

Unlike my previously published monographs, this book was prepared in only a very small part by lectures delivered at conferences or seminars, or articles published in journals. It was developed fully in the context of teaching. The number of students to acknowledge is too big, but I thank all those who approached me with questions of clarification, issues of interest, suggestions, straightforward provocations (during the break of a lecture: 'Why is culture important?'), requests for expansion, and all other forms of either negative or positive criticism. Luckily, the latter substantially outweighed the former. I can say this differently: I thank the majority of students for their commitments.

Preamble: On a Musical Note

Australian magpie[1]

Let us start this introduction with listening – to a bird: the Australian magpie. Considering its sounds as 'singing' or 'music' is an anthropomorphism, with 'anthropomorphism' indicating that people give names to things so as to place them in their own lifeworld, or to 'morph' them according to a human logic. Scholarly speaking – so not spiritually, an issue to which we will come back – the bird, in making its organized sounds, is not communicating with humans. It is sending out something, and listening to what comes back, from its own kind. Biologically speaking, this is clear. Culturally speaking, it is more complicated, for the study of culture implies the study of expression.

1   Wild Ambience, 'Australian Magpie: Song & Calls'.

With regard to this, and in terms of interaction, the question is twofold: do magpies have culture as a result of which they express things that can be understood and learned, also through generations, by members of their own species? And can this exchange of expressions then also be meaningful to others, like other magpie species, or a host of other ones, including the human species?

In what follows, when focusing on cultural interactions, we will start with humans and their cultural interactions. Yet at the end of the explorations, we will also come to consider animal cultures, and technological ones. We do so to counter a too self-evident domination of anthropomorphism. If people define a bird's sounds as 'singing' or as 'music', this is an anthropomorphism. When people describe such 'singing' as a matter of 'competition' or as the marking of a territory, this is an anthropomorphism as well, since the very definition of 'territory' is a human one. Or, to give a third example: the mirror test is yet one other anthropomorphic way of defining whether other beings have a sense of self. Only a small number of species appear to be capable of recognizing themselves in a mirror: chimpanzees, orang-utans, bonobos, Asian elephants, dolphins – and magpies. Yet why would the human mirror be the universal marker of self-recognition or of a sense of self? Suppose that octopuses were the self-proclaimed rulers of the planet. Consequently, they might turn the world into an 'octopomorphic' one. Studying human beings, octopus scholars would ask whether human arms, hands, legs, or feet have their own independent forms of intelligence and agency, for this would be analogous to the intelligence of an octopus. In the perception of octopuses, humans would be limited, if not handicapped, animals: they appear to have a centre of intelligence only in their heads! Recent octopus research even suggests that human beings need a mirror to recognize themselves as a self. Human beings also cannot change the colours and structures of their skin, by the way. They appear to make up for this incapacity by constructing artificial, colourful things with which they cover their skin.

If we come to consider cultural interactions in relation to humans first, and then to animal cultures and the technological ones, this can only be done systematically on the basis of a definition of culture that makes the transition between the three possible. And as the scholarly history of the study of culture proves, it is notoriously difficult to formulate an adequate definition of such a common thing as culture. For instance, a popular study on cultural differences, especially in the world of business – Erin Meyer's *The Culture Map: Breaking Through the Invisible Boundaries of Global Business* (2014) – marks cross-cultural interaction on the basis of eight dominant aspects of cultural habits. These concern, for instance, how people communicate (explicitly vs. implicitly) or evaluate (direct negative feedback vs. indirect negative feedback), how they lead (egalitarian vs. hierarchical), or how they disagree (confrontational vs. avoiding confrontation). Yet Meyer's study does not *define* what is meant by culture.

Another example: in *Understanding Culture: A Handbook for Students in the Humanities*, Babette Hellemans defines culture as 'the sum of the collective **representations** associated with a particular society'.[2] This is a definition, for sure, but one problem here is that culture appears to be something that 'is associated with'. This implies that it can only be assessed from some sort of outside, namely by actors who do the associating. Secondly, culture appears to mark a society. Of course, we should ask what is meant by 'society', then, but the equation of culture with society is in any case a controversial one. In what follows, we will not consider culture to be equivalent to a society. On the contrary, a society may host many cultures (cf. Chapter 4). Finally, we will argue that culture is more than the total sum of collective representations. We will surely deal with the force in representations, but also move beyond them in an attempt to come up with a concise definition of culture as something that people do not only have or use, or associate themselves with, but that they embody and *live* (cf. Chapter 1).

One of the reasons for the difficulty to define culture may be that culture is generally dealt with on the basis of two different manifestations. On the one hand, culture indicates the entire set of practices, expressions, and artefacts by which people organize their lifeworlds. This mode of culture is involved, for example, when people speak of 'Japanese culture', or 'Tapirapé culture' – the culture of one of the indigenous peoples living in Brazil. As the two examples illustrate, scale is not decisive for culture, for we just compared a culture of approximately 126.5 million people with one that currently consists of about two hundred. On the other hand, culture is often used to indicate the entire set of artistic expressions produced by people in fields such as architecture, sculpture, music, literature, cinema, games, and so forth. The two are often distinguished by means of the use of the word 'culture' with a small 'c' and a capital 'C'.

The distinction between culture and Culture connotes a hierarchy that has come to be questioned more and more over the past six decades. One of the issues with this distinction was why, for instance, classical European music would be assigned a capital 'C' and pop music would not; why art house movies would, but by no means television series. Also, why would the

2   Hellemans, *Understanding Culture*, 18. Emphasis in original.

Ghanaian artist and ethnomusicologist Mustafa Tettey Addy be considered as a performer, whereas the French composer and bird watcher Olivier Messiaen (1908-1992) would be blessed with the aura of the capital C, precisely due to his being regarded as a composer. Likewise, why would medieval mystic Hildegard von Bingen's (1098-1179) construction of a secret language for her company of women be a matter of linguistics only, whereas her songs were art? We will return to the issue of cultural hierarchies in Chapters 5 and 8. For now the important point is that the relation between the two, culture and Culture, is pivotal in the field of the humanities for the *forms* that they may use, what these forms express, what such expressive forms can, or may mean; and how such expressions embody a mode of living.

With the heading of this study being 'conflict and cooperation', these two terms need to be defined as well. First of all, in many instances, c/Culture is considered to be a positive matter that brings people together. This is, for instance, what UNESCO, the United Nations Educational, Scientific and Cultural Organization, tells us about culture:

> In today's interconnected world, culture's power to transform societies is clear. Its diverse manifestations – from our cherished historic monuments and museums to traditional practices and contemporary art forms – enrich our everyday lives in countless ways. Heritage constitutes a source of identity and cohesion for communities disrupted by bewildering change and economic instability. Creativity contributes to building open, inclusive and pluralistic societies. Both heritage and creativity lay the foundations for vibrant, innovative and prosperous knowledge societies.[3]

The quote not only entails a contradiction – culture is, on the one hand, a defence against 'bewildering change and economic instability', whereas, on the other hand, it lays the 'foundations for vibrant, innovative and prosperous knowledge societies' – but it also sketches a pretty rosy picture of what culture produces, especially when it is equated with creativity. If the creativity in culture is at the basis of 'open, inclusive, and pluralistic societies', there are as many examples where people have rather creatively produced societies that are, culturally speaking, closed, exclusive, and uniform. Many of the devastating conflicts that people were engaged in, or wilfully have engaged in, were propelled by culture.

We preserve the notion of conflict, in accordance with its etymological origin, for violent confrontations between people. Conflict goes back to

---

3   UNESCO, 'Protecting Our Heritage and Fostering Creativity'.

Latin *confligere*: 'to fight/strike with'. Conflict is different from friction here. Even open, inclusive, and pluralistic societies will brim with frictions. Such frictions can be productive, positive even. They can also be annoying. They may lead to conflict, but not necessarily so.

As for cooperation, historically speaking, there has been much more inter-cultural cooperation than conflict. The reason is simple: people may wage war at times, but they always trade and exchange things, even in times of war. War is temporary, that is; trade and exchange are continuous. Sometimes trade even takes place between warring parties. Cooperation etymologically means 'to work together'. This can be, but need not be work as in modern labour. There are so many ways, also economically, in which people may work together. For instance, the cultural forms of knowledge and practices that women developed with regard to giving birth – also indicated by 'labour' – were developed within cultures but also developed through the help of cultural interactions.[4] One example: currently in Peru healthcare workers who were used to Western ways of giving birth managed to work together with indigenous pregnant women who wanted to give birth according to their customs: sitting upright, with a trusted or loved relative behind them and with a rope in front of them with knots to support themselves.[5] As may be clear, people have tendencies throughout history to mark other cultures as 'other' or 'less'. Nonetheless they have time and again also shown great interest in, or attention for others and other cultures. The human animal may be a pretty brutal one at times, but it is also an attentive and curious creature – or at least it can be.

The book was developed for a second year BA course in international studies. However, it can be useful for other courses, due to its systemic build-up. The book is divided into two blocks. In the first block, culture is studied respectively in terms of larger-scale forms of organization, or realms, such as culture itself, nation-state, world, society, civilization, and community (Chapters 1-6). In this block, culture is defined as such, and cultural interactions are studied for how they relate to politics, to the political, to economies, to affective economies, and to religion. In the second block, forms of self and selfhood are central. There, cultural interactions will be studied respectively in relation to notions of individuality, affiliation, comparability, disability, animality, and technology (Chapters 7-12).

4   See, for instance, Davis-Floyd and Sargent, *Childbirth and Authoritative Knowledge*. As for conflict, next to cooperation, one editor of this volume also worked on a volume in which the effects of economic or military violence on giving birth are central: Scheper-Hughes and Sargent, *Small Wars: The Cultural Politics of Childhood*.
5   Gomez, 'Giving Birth Upright, with Maté'.

Developing the course and writing this book was a learning process in itself. Originally, I was trained in the domain of arts and culture – comparative literature and theory, specifically. My position at the Leiden University Centre for the Arts in Society and at the Department of Film and Literary Studies was the result of this training. At the start of my teaching in The Hague, I tried to translate the knowledge developed in my fields of expertise to a body of students that by and large missed training in the arts and culture and were interested much more in the relevance of cultural dynamics and tensions in the force fields of international, sociopolitical, economic, or religious developments. As will become clear, works of art, literature, films, and music proved to be excellent guides in exploring these international dynamics. Still, I had to recalibrate, reorient, and explore new fields of research, also in response to rapidly developing, planetary developments that involved both human interactions and transhuman ones.

Nothing in what follows is decisive, or conclusive. Almost everything is a matter of scholarly debate, agreement, conversation, or rejection. This does not mean that anything goes. In fact, scholarly speaking, nothing goes. In a scholarly sense, matters only 'go' depending on substantive sensing, analyzing, reasoning, motivating, underpinning, choosing, agreeing, or disagreeing. With regard to the material offered in this text, many of the readers may agree with this or that, others with yet other points; few will agree with nothing. In the field of culture, it is impossible to have a neutral or objective position. Even if this text is an introduction, it is also political in the sense that time and again the question is not just what individuals choose for but also what collectives choose for. In a sense, this introduction is a provocation. It asks readers: what do you choose *for*? Choosing against something is also possible. In my assessment and politically speaking, choosing against something is, in the end, less forceful.

Every chapter consists of two parts that each start with a piece of music as a musical epigraph. The pieces can be either songs with text, or pieces without text. Readers are asked to listen to these before reading the chapter. The reason I wanted to involve music is that it may be the best way to avoid thinking about culture only in terms of 'meaning'. Cultures are as much a matter of rhythms, of choreographies, of movement, of sounds, of all the senses, of which there are more than five.[6] Studying culture is not only

---

6   The Dutch psychiatrist Iris Sommer could easily get to eleven. To test her awareness, she decided to live for a year in Mumbai and the book on this experiment was called *De zeven zintuigen: Over waarnemen en onwaarnemen*, or *The Seven Senses: About Perception and Non Perception*.

something of the scholarly mind, that is. It is as much about sensuous and sensitive perceptiveness since culture is always embodied. Consequently, cultural scholarship that wants to make sense cannot be a matter of the mind only. Cultural knowledge is embodied and positioned knowledge by definition.

Part 1

Cultural Realms

1. Culture in Terms of Representation and as Form-of-life

1.1. In what senses is culture a matter of life and death?

> Señoras y señores
> Buenas tardes, buenas noches
> Buenas tardes, buenas noches
> Señoritas y señores
> To be here with you tonight brings me joy, que alegría
> For this music is my language, and the world es mi familia
> For this music is my language, and the world es mi familia
> For this music is my language
> And the world es mi familia
> For this music is my language...
>
> 'The World Es Mi Familia', from COCO (2017)[1]

In terms of why culture matters and why cultural interactions matter, perhaps the most pronounced and basic question is: in what senses is culture a matter of life and death? Giving an answer to this question forces us to come up with an answer to a second question: what is the definition of culture? To answer both, this chapter explores two pivotal concepts: 'representation' and 'form-of-life'. The two will be dealt with by taking seriously that culture is a matter of life and death, and a matter of representation, or perhaps more than this: a *form*-of-life.

Human beings are not the only animals to have culture (cf. Chapters 11 and 12). Yet for centuries the fact that human beings had or used culture was the dominant marker of difference between them and animals. For instance, the German philosopher Martin Heidegger (1889-1976) stated that only people have a sense of their own mortality because they can think about their inevitable death and express their feelings, anxieties, and desires about it. For sure, animals also die, but according to Heidegger they have no sense beforehand, or no sense of anticipation, that their life is restricted, for this is a culturally determined issue. Leaving aside the issue whether or not animals sense that their life is limited, it is certain

---

1   Molina and Franco, 'The World Es Mi Familia'.

that all cultures make people aware that life is confined within the limits of birth and death.

In general, or fundamentally, human life depends on culture, since it contains the entire set of practices, attitudes, technologies, and artefacts by means of which human beings are able to organize themselves in conflict and cooperation with the living environment. For instance, how to find, prepare, eat, taste, and share food is a matter of culture. The French philosopher Roland Barthes noted that food is a 'system of communication, a body of images, a protocol of usages, situations, and behavior'.[2] With respect to the production, consumption, tasting, and sharing of food, culture is a fundamental issue for the transfer of knowledge between people, collectively and across generations.[3] Here we already have three pivotal elements of a definition of culture. Human beings are a cultivating species; a speaking, communicating, and teaching species; and a sensing and knowing species, be it with several divergences.

For instance, the wisdoms people teach one another with regard to birth, life, and death vary considerably across cultures. The conceptualization of death, the rituals surrounding birth and death, and the practices of dealing with death and the dead differ substantially between, say, Mexican and Maori cultures. More so, even within a particular culture, there will be great differences between individual communities. For instance, in Dutch culture the differences between Muslim, Catholic, Protestant, Jewish, and secular communities are substantial in how they deal with life and death. Moreover, death has come to be dealt with differently with the arrival of consumer culture; or it is being dealt with differently in the current phase of global capitalism.

In the context of global capitalism, with its roots in the period of colonialism and the flows it has produced, some speak of a 'necropolitics', as Cameroonian political theorist Achille Mbembe did.[4] Mbembe used the term to indicate that the organization of life and death is not only a cultural concern, but a governmental and legal issue as well, in a situation that Mbembe describes as perpetual war. We will return to the relation between culture and politics in the next two chapters. For now, the point is that Mbembe highlighted how in many current circumstances political and legal actors decide who is to die and who is to live. The cases of immigrants

2   Barthes, 'Toward a Psychosociology of Contemporary Food Consumption', 24.
3   On the cultural and social simultaneity of the senses, also in terms of knowledge, when dealing with food and eating, see Mol, *Eating in Theory*.
4   Mbembe, 'Necropolitics'.

trying to cross the Mexican borders or the Mediterranean seas are just two chilling examples.

In most cases and most cultures, life will be valued more than death. Still, many cultures define situations in which death is valued more than life, whether for spiritual reasons or out of shame. In terms of politics and legality, however, the question is who is allowed to live, or for whom authorities will take responsibility. As we will see, politics is distinguishable from culture, here, but also closely connected to it.

The *value* that people attach to their culture is not fixed. They may assimilate into another culture, or combine elements from different cultures to design a new mixture that feels like their own. The Dutch, for instance, are famous for their tulips nowadays. Yet the cultivation of tulips came from Turkey – *tulipa* originally means 'flower resembling a turban'. The story is that in the seventeenth century, some tulip bulbs that the sultan had presented as a precious gift to a Flemish diplomat, ended up being passed on to a Leiden professor named Carolus Clusius, from whose house they were later stolen. Consequently, an entire new industry started that redefined the Dutch self-image. The same scientist, under whose supervision the *hortus botanicus* (botanical garden) was created in Leiden, also introduced potatoes, tobacco, tomatoes, beans, and maize into the Low Countries. For centuries, potatoes were another Dutch icon, captured in an equally iconic painting by Vincent van Gogh: *The Potato Eaters* (1885).

Another example: Russians can be proud to be Russian, yet that very name is adopted from the Vikings, who were called *Rus*, and who in the eighth century had settled in the region stretching from the Baltic sea to the Black Sea. The Vikings, in turn, were originally much opposed to Christianity but assimilated into Christian culture nevertheless over the course of four centuries, which is why all Nordic countries in Europe are now by and large Protestant. All of this is ample evidence, then, that people can be irreverent, flexible, and innovative in their dealing with culture.

There is also ample evidence of how culture may be so quintessential to human beings that they cling to it as if it were life itself. People have been willing to give their lives for a culture, or a religion, either because they refused to give in to a suppressive power or because they were willing to give their life for the greater good – something coined as 'altruistic suicide'. All martyrs can be considered as an example, here. The explanation may be that life without culture is not possible. One of the horrors of the transatlantic slave trade was not just that human beings were enslaved, but that they were robbed of their culture and meaningful lifeworld. Yet despite this deprivation, they started to reshape their lives culturally in the new enforced circumstances. The reason was that life without culture is, indeed, not possible, or not bearable. At the same time, for enslaved people the culture of origin held a palpable attraction for decades, and even centuries.

In this context, the African-American philosopher bell hooks – whose refusal to spell her name with capitals is intentional – was interested in pedagogy and didactics in *Teaching to Transgress* (1994) or *Teaching Community: A Pedagogy of Hope* (2004). She feels herself to be a part of a long tradition of people who had to teach themselves how to organize their own culture against oppressive forces in such a way that they felt alive, valuable, and meaningful. Here, hooks noticed the enormous powers residing in representation. These powers reside in two manifestations. If people belong to a certain culture, everything they do, whether they want to or not, expresses this culture. The ways in which people walk, talk, belch, and decorate their environments, the ways in which they have sex, dress, eat, or hold their head; they all express a certain culture. In whatever they do, people represent a culture, then, or they embody different cultures – whether they want it or not. The realm of representation also contains all the explicit ways by means of which a culture is expressed, or by means of which people are given the task to represent something. If people are appointed to be ambassador for Mozambique in China, for instance, they represent their country, but also its culture(s).

As the prefix re-suggests, representation is a manifestation of something else. Philosopher and literary scholar Gayatri Chakravorty Spivak made a distinction in this context between representation as *Vertretung* or as *Darstellung*.[5] The first means that representations or representatives are representing something or someone else. The second, *Darstellung*, concerns all those case in which something is being *expressed*, or posited by means of representation. In both cases we encounter the loop of culture. Most CEOs, for instance, will not accept an old, second-hand, and creaky kitchen table as their desk. They will want an impressive, massive, solid, big, and shiny table, with one chair at the head. This table and the organization of space that it implies, represents a specific distribution of power, and suggests that the CEO has real power that is represented through the table. Yet it also works the other way around, for what would the CEO be without it, or without a salary, without the dress or the suit, without the contract? More generally, the paradox

---

5   Spivak, *The Post-Colonial Critic*, 108.

here is that any culture uses multiple sets of representations, but at the same time the entire set of representations also embodies that culture. It is not the case that there is some entity of 'culture' that comes first, and is then represented. Culture is present only, or posited, through representations. This is why the struggle about what is being represented is so immensely charged.

In this context, hooks noticed the nigh unstoppable force residing in movies, as powerful instruments of cultural representation that influence the ways in which people think, feel, and sense. This was partly a matter of who was or was not being represented on the screen, but, more importantly, of how people were being represented. In the context of the United States of America, it concerned a movie industry with its own aesthetic and political agendas and its own people in charge. Still, any kind of political power has always been invested in this force of representation, and for good reason. The first Jesuits who came to South America had well-developed programmes to teach indigenous peoples to sing Christian songs. Currently, the Chinese government is very capable of suppressing any form of cultural expression in the north-western part of China where the Uighurs live. Aside from political oppression, or lethal violence, the Chinese government developed massive and intensive teaching programmes to make the Uighur people give up their own culture and to make them culturally Chinese.

Situations like these may drive people to a point where they would rather die than give up on what organizes their lives meaningfully, affectively, and sensibly: their own culture. This does not mean they desire to die, although this can also happen, but that they are willing to risk their life in a struggle or battle for their own culture. Mahatma Gandhi took this risk, for instance. Yet his murderer also did so. The latter was a Hindu nationalist who considered Gandhi's agreement to the separation of India and Pakistan to be too favourable to Muslims. He was willing to sacrifice his own life in the fight for a dominant Hindu culture. He knew he would be captured, having killed Ghandi in a crowd at broad daylight, tried, and sentenced to death. And so it happened.

To many, culture will not be experienced as a matter of life and death on an everyday basis. People simply live their culture. The latter phrase may seem odd. Do people not *have* a culture? In the next part of this chapter, when answering the question of how to define culture, we will make a scholarly decision to reject this idea of people 'having' a culture. A culture is not a car. It is a form-of-life; people live it, and this is why they are so attached to it.

We started this chapter with the song 'The World Es Mi Familia', from the animation movie COCO (2016). Its lyrics were written by Adrian Molina and the music by composer Germaine Franco, a Latino and American of Mexican descent. The movie deals with the most famous days of festivity in Mexico, Día de muertos, on 1-2 November. For those not familiar with this festival, the movie is just a fiction that is entertaining. To Mexicans, it may mean much more. They do not simply *know* the festival; they live it. The song goes like this:

> Señoras y señores
> Buenas tardes, buenas noches
> Buenas tardes, buenas noches
> Señoritas y señores
> To be here with you tonight brings me joy, que alegría
> For this music is my language, and the world es mi familia
> For this music is my language, and the world es mi familia
> For this music is my language
> And the world es mi familia
> For this music is my language...[6]

Textually, the song embodies a cultural interaction between an English language/USA culture and a Spanish language/Mexican culture. This interaction becomes evident given that two languages are mixed in one sentence, as in 'the world es mi familia'. The latter phrase makes it sound as if the boy considers the whole world to be his family, which gives it a harmonious touch. Yet the cultural meanings and connotations of 'family' differ substantially across cultures, ranging from a nuclear family with father, mother and two kids, to large and flexible groups of relatives, which need not even be related by blood. As for the harmony within families, all readers can decide whether families are only about harmony and cooperation or whether there may be considerable conflicts involved. As for the concept world, we will be discussing it in Chapter 3 and then conclude that assuming the world to be one may be the wrong way of looking at it.

For now, the most important thing is that the song clearly indicates that culture is always related to collectives, from relatively small to bigger ones. This will be the focus of the first six chapters. Let us therefore consider in the next part of this chapter, how culture can be defined as a collective endeavour; and let us choose how to define culture.

---

6   Molina and Franco, 'The World Es Mi Familia', cf. note 1.

1.2.   What is the definition of culture?

> All the people in the world are dreaming (get up stand up)
> Some of us cry for the rights of survival (get up stand up)
> Saying c'mon c'mon! Stand up for your rights (get up stand up)
> While others don't give a damn
> They're all waiting for a perfect day
> You better get up and fight for your rights
> Don't be afraid of the move you make
> You better listen to your tribal voice!
>
> 'Tribal Voice' by Yothu Yindi (1991)[7]

In the field of cultural studies, so-called objective ways of studying or, say, measuring culture, are possible, but the question is how meaningful these methods are. Consider, for instance, the visas that the Australian Department of Immigration and Border Protection hands out, requesting applicants to confirm they understand that:

> Australian society values respect for the freedom and dignity of the individual, freedom of religion, commitment to the rule of law, Parliamentary democracy, equality of men and women and a spirit of egalitarianism that embraces mutual respect, tolerance, fair play and compassion for those in need and pursuit of the public good. Australian society values equality of opportunity for individuals, regardless of their race, religion or ethnic background.[8]

Scholars from the University of Western Australia then wondered: would these values indeed be subscribed to by Australians? They organized an inquiry to which 7000 people replied; the results revealed that power, achievements, and traditions are not at the top of the list of Australians' values. Instead, they value benevolence, security, and societal universalism highly.[9] These values are specified as:

> People who value benevolence would strive to be loyal, dependable, honest, helpful, kind, and forgiving. [...] Individuals who value security

7   Yindi, 'Tribal Voice'.
8   Values Project, 'What Are Australian Values?'
9   Ibid.

deem social order, national security, and their family's (and own personal)
security to be very important. [...] People who value universalism in a
society, attach great importance to equality, social justice, tolerance,
wisdom and peace in the world.[10]

Given this, one would surely love to meet Australians. Yet the passages
quoted and paraphrased, above all, show the limitations of so-called
empirical data in the cultural domain. For how representative are the
7000 who participated? How many Aboriginals replied, for instance; and
would they agree that 'equality, social justice, tolerance, wisdom and peace
in the world' are the backbone of Australian culture? Would they feel they
were being dealt with benevolently? And then, though Australia does
not collect statistics on the ethnic origins of its residents, it asks people
to specify their ancestries during each census. In 2016, 16.5% of Australians identified themselves as East Asian, Southeast Asian, or Central and
Southern Asian. Did they respond to the survey? If so, would they have
preferred Australian culture over their culture of origin? And just one more
question: if Australians prioritize security, the question is whose security
this is, or in how far the longing for security by some is compatible with
universal benevolence.

With culture, we are in the diverse and, at times, disparate realm of histories, situations, and positions with different values that people are, or *feel
to be*, attached to. We approach this complex field inevitably with our own
cultural background. This is why any empirical evidence is always framed by
positions or situations from which people collected and interpreted it. The
values mentioned above, moreover, illustrate that culture is not something
people simply *have*, but that it is dear to them, *drives* them, and shapes
their lifeworlds. You cannot 'have' benevolence, for instance; you have to
embody, practice, and enact it. The Australian example also makes it clear
that there are no pure cultures. Australia only seems to be an exceptional
migratory country here. Generally, human beings are a migratory species.
The history of Europe is one relentless dynamic of migration. In this context,
the nineteenth-century nation-state's desire to discipline or purify national
cultures becomes close to an anomaly. Still, the very construction of the
nation-state, and the passions involved, demonstrate once more that cultures
are not rational constructs. They are a matter of affect.

Affect will be dealt with in more depth later (cf. Chapter 5). For now,
literature helps us to understand what is meant by it. Ever since the

---

10   Ibid.

Second World War, Dutch history has included the history of the so-called Dutch Moluccans; some 15,000 family members of 3500 soldiers who had served in the Dutch colonial army and were expelled from Indonesia in 1950. Their arrival in the Netherlands was a shameful affair, since they were not welcomed into Dutch society but were stowed away in separate and isolated camps. The painful results of this cultural exclusion became evident during the decades that followed. Sylvia Pessireron, daughter of first-generation migrants, addressed this in novels published between 1998 and 2014 that carried titles such as *Closed Trunks, The Silenced Soldier, Moluccans in the Netherlands: We Came Here on Orders* and *Between People and Ghosts.*[11] In an interview, Pessireron stated: 'Yes, the pain of your parents – and you can only feel it. They do not talk about it – perhaps this is the worst' (my translation). Apparently, this pain is something that determines the parents' lives, is present always, though not expressed, as an undercurrent that defines all relations, also with their children.[12] It is a matter of affect that is prior to language, or that can block language. On an everyday basis it may lead to emotions of sadness, anger, depression, and confusion. Affectively speaking, *knowing* the history of the Dutch Moluccans is not enough, consequently; what matters is to feel it, to sense and understand it, and to acknowledge the pain embodied in it.

In many definitions of culture, the intrinsically relational aspect of affect is missing. For instance, the *Oxford English Dictionary (OED)* defines "culture" as:

> 1. The arts and other manifestations of human intellectual achievement regarded collectively; 2. The ideas, customs, and social behaviour of a particular people or society; 2.1. The attitudes and behavior characteristic of a particular social group.[13]

In this case, culture with a capital 'C' is mentioned first, and the lower-case culture comes second. And if the dictionary opts for 'intellectual achievement', then feelings, emotions, or affects do not play a decisive role in either case.

---

11   Pessiseron, *Gesloten koffers, De verzwegen soldaat, Molukkers in Nederland* and *Tussen mensen en geesten.*
12   On the expressive force of silence in the Dutch Moluccan context, see Engelenhoven, "'Whereof One Cannot Speak...'".
13   *Oxford English Dictionary*, s.v. 'Culture'.

Anthropologist Clifford Geertz (1926-2006) came closer to an adequate definition of culture when he used a definition by sociologist Alfred Weber to describe culture as follows:

> Since man is 'an animal suspended in webs of significance he himself has spun', I take culture to be those webs, and the analysis of it to be therefore not an experimental science in search of laws but an interpretive one in search of meaning.[14]

The fragment in quotation marks is Weber's, and it is, culturally speaking, telling that Geertz's definition incorporates what he learned from someone else. As for the definition of culture itself, Geertz distinctly defines mankind as an animal species. This emphasizes not so much intellectual achievement, but rather drives and impulses. Secondly, culture is seen to be palpably made by and done to people, given that it suspends them in a self-made web. This web metaphor is affectively charged – one can feel its push and pull. Thirdly, culture is not about applying objective natural laws or discovering them by means of experiments, but a search for significance, meaning, and interpretation as a matter of sense.

Still, Geertz's definition is highly metaphorical. I endeavour to be more precise and will take my cue from a concept proposed by the philosopher Ludwig Wittgenstein (1889-1951), which was subsequently politicized by the Italian philosopher Giorgio Agamben. The latter, in a study on early medieval communities of monks, noticed that these monks replaced notions of possession – of what one *has* – with what is used or practiced: something one *does*. In doing so, they shaped a form of life that existed counter to and relatively independent from political power. It was a life, moreover, that did not exist separately from its form. Form and life were one: a form-of-life. David Kishik's study on the concept has shown that form-of-life has always been observed from two sides: 'the first view focuses on the unity and necessity of the human form of life as a given that persists over time, the opposite view emphasizes the diversity and contingency of different human forms and the ability to alter such conventions.'[15] This is analogous to the ambiguity addressed in the previous part of this chapter. On the one hand, people have proven to be extremely flexible to adapt themselves culturally, or to innovate. On the other hand, they have been willing to give their lives for the preservation of their culture.

14   Geertz, *The Interpretation of Cultures*, 5.
15   Kishik, *Wittgenstein's Form of Life*, 121-122.

Now, Agamben defined form-of-life in opposition to the modern political organization of society. According to him, modern politics is a form of politics that starts with the invention of sovereignty as supreme state power. This state power takes as its point of departure unprotected, naked life, in order to organize this life politically in the way it wants to. Most people will feel that the life of a newly born baby is valuable as such, for instance. But what happens if the state does not grant or guarantee this newborn child citizenship; or when the state defines it as an inferior being that resides on the level of plague animals? Then either this child becomes illegal and is without full protection of the state, or it can be actively destroyed by the state, as happened with Gypsy or Jewish children in the Nazi period. The difference between the two forms of life is captured by the difference between the Greek terms *zoë* and *bios*: between a life shared by all beings and a politically disciplined form of life.

Counter to this politically organized form, Agamben posited an autonomous form-of-life, which would be a 'happy form of life' that ' should be rather, an absolutely profane 'sufficient life' that has reached the perfection of its own power and its own communicability – a life over which sovereignty and right no longer have any hold."[6] What Agamben proposes here, implies that an organized form of life is valuable in itself and does not depend on the acknowledgment of the state. Opposed to the sovereign power of the state, he proposes another kind of sovereign life that has reached the perfection of its own power.

It would not do justice to the very notion of culture if we define it in terms of perfection. Yet culture is a communicable form in its own right, that in origin is formed by a bottom-up organization of life that is not immediately defined by power. The Dutch historian Johan Huizinga even stated that culture has its origin in play, which may also explain that there is an arbitrary element to cultural forms.[17] More important for now is that, *basically*, culture does not find its source in power but can be considered better in terms of empowerment.

As Geertz noted, culture is a self-woven web in which people come to be entangled. Such culture webs can exist prior to politics. Obviously, they exert their own power. For instance, the play that Huizinga talked about would have to be solidified in rules at some point that define a form-of-life. Yet culture, basically, cannot be *reduced* to power, though it certainly can and will be *used* by powers. A paradigmatic example is the monastic

16   Agamben, *Means without End*, 114-115.
17   Huizinga, *Homo Ludens*. Originally published in 1938.

community of women that Hildegard von Bingen realized in the twelfth
century in the Rhineland – a case that Agamben tellingly did not deal with.
Von Bingen and her followers managed to do this against all the odds, in
the context of the patriarchal powers of the Catholic Church. Monks, as
men, had always been implicated in the political game, and their attempt
to organize their own life was less of a leap of faith. Women did not have
that privilege. Nevertheless, they built forth on, and established their own
cultural existence in a community that lived its own form-of-life. This proves
the point again that culture, in first instance, is made bottom-up. There was
not, once, a fully developed body of culture that had already existed. Or it
consisted in part but that part was made into a new form.

The making of a life worth living in contemporary circumstances was
defined by the French philosopher Henri Lefebvre as a matter of *autoges-
tion*.[18] This as well was a term which indicates that a form of life is made
bottom-up. Elsewhere Lefebvre's phrased it like this: 'A real culture is at once
a mode of living, a way of thinking and an ability to act. It is a sentiment
of life incorporated in a human community.'[19] In a study called *Cultural
Complexity* the anthropologist Ulf Hannerz used the concept 'form of life'
to indicate a specific aspect of contemporary life in general – next to, for
instance, the state, the market, or social movements.[20] With form of life,
Hannerz meant subcultural interactions at the most local level. Instead of
taking the nation-state as a marker of cultural identity, he focused again
on the many ways in which peoples themselves form their lives culturally.

All the aspects considered above have brought me to the following
definition of culture:

> Culture is a form-of-life, embodied in how collectives of beings performa-
> tively shape all aspects of their life and world, in communal existence, as
> a distinct, partly arbitrary, affectively charged, meaningful expression
> that is transferable through time and space, that can produce change,
> can resist change, or can cope with change.

Through the terms 'form' and 'shape' both media and representations are
implied. Forms can only be shaped in and through media, and it is only
through these that representations can come to exist. As for both media

---

18   See Lefebvre, *The Urban Revolution* and *State, Space, World*.
19   Merrifield, *Henri Lefebvre*, 160. The original can be found in Henri Lefebvre, *La somme et le
reste*, vol. 2 (Paris: La nef de Paris, 1959).
20   Hannerz, *Cultural Complexity*.

and representations, the definition concerns much more than Culture with a capital C; the latter simply indicates the ways in which media (language, paint, space, sound, etc.) are explored to the fullest in their potential to express being. Culture is part and parcel of culture, that is.

'Performatively', meanwhile, does not indicate the theatrical or dramatic. The term is derived from speech act theory, indicating instances when people simultaneously do what they say, like when they say: 'I promise'. In promising something people are both saying and doing just this: they perform the act of promising. Translated to the realm of human behaviour, or culture, the performative suggests that a culture becomes what people repeatedly express in their actions and doings.[21] For instance, if people repeatedly, or always, take off their shoes before entering the house, this activity becomes an expression of their culture. No prior essence, say 'politeness', is then merely expressed through this act. Culture is not an indication of the essence of people but of what people do, repeatedly and recurrently. Still, this repetition then comes to be experienced as a matter of essence for that culture.

As for the 'partly arbitrary', this indicates that there is not an absolute necessity that defines what becomes a cultural expression. In Indian culture, for instance, the cow is holy; in Jewish and Islamic cultures, people do not eat pork. Yet in some cultures, cows are a matter of food and cows' eyes may be a delicacy. Likewise, in some cultures the so-called cooked or roasted suckling pigs (piglets between two or six weeks old) are a delicacy to be enjoyed. To be sure: within a culture people will argue that the choice for one or the other is essential. On a meta-level, however, the arbitrary nature is evident. Otherwise, all cultures would prohibit the consumption of pork or declare cows to be holy. Reality proves otherwise. On a more conceptual level, the very fact that culture consists by means of representations is at the heart of its arbitrary quality. In making representations, arbitrary innovation is key. For instance, if all cultures deal with notions of divinity, the cultural representations of divinity will differ immensely.

We started this part of the chapter with the song 'Tribal Voice', by an Australian band called Yothu Yindi: Child and Mother. This is a band that consists of constantly interchanging musicians of aboriginal and *balanda* – that is, of non-aboriginal, or European-Australian – descent. Its most famous singer died in 2013 and, although his name should no longer be mentioned according to aboriginal cultural custom, his family gave consent to show his

---

21   The transition from speech act theory to human behavior and identity was made by Judith Butler in *Gender Trouble*.

work. Perhaps music is the best example to indicate the difference between representation and form-of-life. People do not only experience music, or listen to it, or interpret it; they do it, are moved by it and dance to it.

We will now delve deeper into the relation between culture and politics, and between culture and the political in the next two chapters. Correspondingly, we will deal with the nineteenth-century model of the nation-state that has become so self-evident globally. The first question is: in what sense is culture a matter of politics itself and how was and is culture used by politics?

2. Culture and Politics: The Paradox of Self-Determination and the Nation-state

2.1. Self-determination: Self-evident or a paradox?

Jutros mi je ruza procvetala
Ruzu gledam pa sam zaplakala
Ruzo moja mladost sam ti dala
Svojom sam te suzom zalivala

Kol'ko sam te puta poljubila
Jos pupoljak mladi dok si bila
Ispijala rosu s tvojih grana
Mesto usne mojega dragana

Moj je dragi otis'o davno
Ja ga cekam vec godinu ravno
Ruzu gledam na te mislim dragi
Na te usne, na tvoj pogled blagi

'Jutros Mi Je Ruza Procvjetala' by Amira Medunjanin (2004)[1]

In this chapter we will first deal with the relation between culture and politics, and in the subsequent chapter with the relation between culture and the political. For now, we focus on how culture may be a matter of politics itself, and how culture was, is, or can be used by politics. In recent centuries, one of the most dominant ways in which culture was used by politics was for the construction of the nation-state. This construction was very much propelled by the idea of self-determination. Yet, as proved to be the case fairly early on, the very idea of the determination of a collective self often entailed the forced integration, the silent subjection, expulsion

1   Medunjanin, 'Jutros Mi Je Ruza Procvjetala'. The song is used in the project 'From Woman to Woman' ('Od Zene do Zene'), in cooperation with the group Musicians without Borders and the Bosnian women's organization Snaga Žene (Strength of a Woman). For the music, see: https://www.youtube.com/watch?v=-ybWolswXUU.

or destruction of others. Telling examples, here, are all the indigenous peoples inhabiting the Americas – North and South. If Walt Whitman (1819-1892) sings about the young United States of America: 'These States are the amplest poem, / Here is not merely a nation, but a teeming nation of nations',[2] the indigenous people that were forced to live in these states were certainly *nations*, but could not co-determine what route the new nation-state was going to take. Put differently, in some senses the legitimate construction of nation-states involved considerable conflicts and crimes, and does so until today. As a result, the so-called international community has had to solve vexing legal problems. One question is, for instance: how can such conflicts be solved? Another one is: how can such crimes be punished?

As for the first, the Kurds may be a good case in point. In the context of the colonial appropriation of the Middle East by two European colonial powers, the United Kingdom and France, the entire Middle East was artificially cut up into parts. The secret Sykes-Picot Agreement of 1916 was at the basis of this – supported by the Russian Empire (on its last feet) and the Kingdom of Italy (soon to be a fascist state and later a republic). Moreover, both the colonial powers of the United Kingdom and France would collapse within decades. Still, the two colonial powers on the way out reorganized an entire region, as a result of which the Kurds were left in no man's land as a nation and would come to be dispersed over four different territories: Iran, Iraq, Syria, and Turkey. In all these countries Kurds live in conflict with ruling parties. How is this going to be solved? None of the four artificially created nation-states is willing to accept a separate Kurd state.

Internationally, the world's two most important international courts of justice in The Hague are concerned with the construction of nation-states or their behaviour in terms of conflicts and crimes. The International Court of Justice, which convenes in the iconic building referred to as the Peace Palace, is the principal judicial organ of the United Nations and primarily concerned with solving conflicts. The International Criminal Court (ICC), hosted in a remarkable though less iconic building, is underpinned by an assembly of individual nation-states. With the Statute of Rome, the states that support this court announced it in 1998 and had it officially established in 2002. The ICC investigates 'and, where warranted, tries individuals charged with the gravest crimes of concern to the international community: genocide, war crimes, crimes against humanity and the crime of aggression'.[3]

---

2   Whitman, 'By Blue Ontario's Shore'.
3   International Criminal Court, 'About the Court'.

The list of countries that accept the authority of this court is vast but also includes considerable gaps, such as the United States of America, Russia, and China. The first two did sign but withdrew their signature; the third never participated at all.

This refusal to take part in the ICC is both politically and culturally motivated. The very nature of the International Criminal Court implies that it cannot be culturally specific. Rather, it should be able to investigate and judge how culture has been used for political purposes in a criminal way. As we speak, for instance, the Chinese government is actively and forcefully destroying the culture of the Uighur people in the north-west of the country. This is a case that might be investigated by the ICC. Yet no Chinese officials can ever be brought before the ICC court because China does not acknowledge its authority.

One of the driving factors in the establishment the ICC was a set of civil wars that raged from 1991 to 2001 in what was, until its dissolution in 1992, the Socialist Federal Republic of Yugoslavia. These civil wars led to Yugoslavia's division into the independent states of Macedonia, Serbia, Montenegro, Bosnia and Herzegovina, Croatia, and Slovenia. The civil wars were brutal and criminal in several respects. The ICC did not exist at the time and a separate tribunal was organized. The International Criminal Tribunal for the former Yugoslavia was in service between 1993 and 2017, judging criminal cases involving horrifying atrocities that were almost all culturally motivated. The court also had to assess whether genocide had taken place or not.

Indeed, if a people's self-determination can lead to the establishment of their own state, the dark flipside of this programme can also be the destruction of peoples. The term 'genocide' etymologically refers to the Greek term γένος (*génos*), cognate with Latin *gens*; both words denote race, kind, tribe, or clan. The *-cide* part means killing or killer. The term was coined by the Polish-Jewish lawyer Raphael Lemkin who studied the destruction of the Armenian and Jewish people. If *gens* emphasizes the involvement of a people, the question, of course, is what marks a collective entity as 'a people'. It is impossible to consider such marking without culture.

In the case of Yugoslavia, for instance, both Croatian and Serbian politicians vilified the Muslim culture of peoples living in Bosnia and Herzegovina or those of Albanians living in Kosovo. Yet during the Second World War, Croatian fascists had also committed genocide on Serbs, whom they considered to be culturally inferior. The Ustaše, a fascist and ultranationalist organization active in Croatia between 1929 and 1945, had its roots in the nineteenth century but was also much influenced by Nazi ideas about the cultural superiority or inferiority of certain groups. All of this was echoed during the civil wars of the 1990s.

Wars such as those in Yugoslavia provoke the question of how they are propelled by culturally determined affects that are either used politically or are politically motivated. To be able to answer this question, we need a definition of politics. Etymologically, the term 'politics' goes back to the Greek term *polis*, and therefore denotes a certain collective once again; a body of citizens organized around an administrative centre. However, it would be wrong to simply translate *polis* as *city* or *city-state*. A classical Greek city-state was surrounded by an agricultural area that provided the city with the necessary food. This region and the people living in it were part of the city-state. A *polis* is marked, then, by a body of citizens that consists of groups with different functions and alternating interests. Politics comes into being when these groups decide to regulate the distribution of power in such a way that differences of interest can be negotiated peacefully, even if this may involve fierce struggles.

In defining politics, I take my cue from several sources, such as the English political theorist Bernard Crick, who drew a sharp distinction between politics and other types of power or rule. This is already one important aspect of the definition of politics. Politics is not simply a matter of the execution of power. Any brute can do that. Politics is a matter of a regulated and distributed form of power. A second important point was addressed by feminist thinker Angela Davis, who argued in *Women, Culture & Politics* (1989) that racial and gender relations in daily life are also a matter of power and politics.[4] In this context politics is clearly not a realized ideal distribution of power, since there is always a struggle going on. Rather, it is about how to regulate and distribute the execution of power itself. The second important thing to note, then, is that politics is about negotiating frictions, disagreements, and imbalances. A third source of inspiration is the work of the Argentinian philosopher Enrique Dussel, who, in a text called *Twenty Theses on Politics*, developed the idea that politics has a positive ground in the material conditions that allow a people to establish their lives.[5] Here the important point is that politics is not instrumental but concerns the ways in which people are able to organize their own lifeworlds.

There is an intrinsic political aspect to culture itself, here, as it is always also a matter of regulation. In many cultures, for instance, the food one

4   Davis, *Women, Culture & Politics*.
5   The original title was *20 tesis de política*, from 2006. It was translated as *Twenty Theses on Politics*.

should or should not eat is a matter of regulation. The same holds for the clothes one should wear, or how women and men should dress. This is why culture has been considered to be a prefiguration of any form of political and legal order. Issues of regulation also concern, or intersect with, matters such as the roles cast on different generations or those between human beings and animals. As for gender, one of the consistent riddles for feminists was why, in so many cultures, the roles assigned to men and women respectively were hierarchized on the basis of a scale of superiority and inferiority. In the European context, for instance, once a man and a woman married, the woman had to give up her last name, which was determined by the father, because she now belonged to another male family line.

Even if cultures express and embody distinct power structures, culture per se is pre-political. As soon as power becomes a matter of negotiating the differences in a regulated way, with the participation of all parties involved, it becomes a matter of politics and its aim will either be to preserve the status quo or to change things. In fact, almost all battles for freedom concern the opening up of an enclosed space of power into one of negotiations and promised openness: a space of doing politics.

Still, if the dynamic between a closed and open system of power-distribution is central to all struggles for self-determination, we encounter a pivotal paradox. If, for instance, the Serbs claimed and still claim the right to live independently in their own territory, this also implies that others could or cannot live there. Thus, opening up a space of one's own also entails the closing down of that space for others.

One could defend such closure with arguments, but culture is not a matter of arguments. Culturally speaking, the closure of a political space is almost always linked to sheer power that often finds a discursive underpinning in a mythical moment in history that becomes culturally and affectively charged (cf. Chapter 3). In the case of Serbia, the mythical historical moment during their struggle for self-determination is the day of the Battle of Kosovo, dated 1389, between the Serbian and Ottoman armies. The battle took place on 28 June (15 June in the calendar of the Serbian Orthodox Church) which also happened to be Vidovdan, or St. Vitus' Day. Over the course of several centuries, this date turned into a matter of performative repetition. Serbia used this day to declare war on the Ottoman Empire in 1876. Serbia signed a secret alliance with Austria-Hungary on this day in 1881. The assassination of Archduke Franz Ferdinand of Austria by the Serbian Gavrilo Princip, which would start the First World War, took place on this day, in 1914. In 1921, on this day, Serbian King Alexander I proclaimed the Vidovdan Constitution. Finally, the 600th anniversary of the battle was honoured by a so-called battle speech by the leader of the Republic of Serbia, Slobodan Milošević, on 28 June 1989. This speech would be a pivotal step in the process leading up to Yugoslavia's civil war.

Both Serbian and Croatian politicians, during the Yugoslavian civil wars, aimed to establish more or less ethnically and culturally homogenous nation-states. The Republic of Bosnia and Herzegovina was a stumbling block in this endeavour. Here a mixed populace of 40% Muslim Bosnians, 32% Serbs, and 17% Croats had lived together for centuries. The leaders of Serbia and Croatia, Milošević (1941-2006) and Tuđman (1922-1999), secretly agreed to invade the Republic of Bosnia and Herzegovina and to subsequently share the territory. At that moment the international political force field made its presence felt. Under the umbrella of the United Nations, Bosnia and Herzegovina's independence was safeguarded; although it took years of war and would include the lasting trauma of the taking of Srebrenica by Serbian forces and the inability of Dutch troops to prevent a mass killing of around 8000 Muslim Bosnians.

The epigraph for this part of the chapter was taken from 'Roses for Srebrenica', a song by Amira Medunjanin, that was used by Musicians without Borders and the Bosnian women's organization Snaga Žene. The volunteer organization, Musicians without Borders, focuses on music to heal traumas and wants to help people connect despite overwhelming forces of violence and war. Their aim is to reconcile people, which is certainly possible. Yet will they be able to come together, truly, across borders? To answer this question, we have to delve into the global dominance of the nation-state, its fixed borders, and the way in which its global dominance is a nasty heritage of colonialism.

2.2.   Why is the nation-state culturally determined?

> Thou art the ruler of the minds of all people,
> Dispenser of India's destiny.
> The name rouses the hearts of Punjab, Sind, Gujarat and Maratha,
> Of the Dravid and Orissa and Bengal;
> It echoes in the hills of the Vindhyas and Himalayas,
> Mingles in the music of the Yamuna and Ganga
> And is chanted by the waves of the Indian Sea.
> They pray for thy blessings and sing thy praise.
> The salvation of all people is in thy hand,

Thou dispenser of India's destiny.
Victory, victory, victory to thee.

Rabindranath Tagore, 'India's National Anthem' (1911)[6]

If politics concerns the regulated distribution of power in such a way that differences of interest can be negotiated within a body politic, this exposes the paradox discussed in the previous part, namely that self-determination may imply the expulsion of others. In a relatively open political field, it is possible that different cultural groups are able or allowed to negotiate their differences, and to take part in the distribution of power. However, it may also be the case that people do not feel that the way in which they want to organize their lives is being done justice. They may decide to form a separate entity, one that is more closed off, more of their own, and politics then nurtures this closure. In fact, the way in which the international force field of politics is organized depends on this closure in the shape of individual and sovereign nation-states. How does culture relate to this dynamic of closing down and opening up political bodies? To answer this question, we have to distinguish between nation and state.

Originally, 'state' means nothing other than condition, or circumstance. This meaning can be traced in phrases like: 'Look at the state of you.' Yet this simple definition took on legal overtones once the question became: what kind of state are entities or subjects in, in terms of power? At that moment hierarchy comes into the debate in order to define the term. 'State' came to denote a claim of power of one's own, over or against others. During the sixteenth and seventeenth centuries, when Europe was torn apart by all sorts of wars, including civil wars propelled by social, political, and religious frictions, the English philosopher Thomas Hobbes introduced the state as the supreme power that could safeguard people against this destructive dynamic. To imagine its protective powers, he came up with a story. In accordance with their nature, so he claimed, people were constantly fighting with one another. This is why they needed an artificial construct, the state, to safeguard them from each other. Hobbes' story became one of the most repeated and successful political fictions ever. As a result of this success, the artificial nation-state acquired the status of nigh being natural, as a result of which it does not appear to have an alternative. Moreover, whereas Hobbes introduced the state to counter a violence he defined as 'natural',

---

6   Lyrics and music by Rabindranath Tagore; music based on a traditional Brahmo hymn. 'India's National Anthem' was first publicly recited on 27 December 1911.

in the coming centuries the newly created nation-states would engage in massive forms of war, world wars even, and would develop a colonial system that was intrinsically aggressive and violent.

Indeed, it is hard to imagine the international status quo without the nation-state. Yet it is a fairly recent invention, and came to be realized fully only since the nineteenth century as a particularly European phenomenon. The nation-state fuses a political notion, the state, with a cultural one: the nation. The *Oxford English Dictionary* (*OED*) defines nation as 'an extensive aggregate of persons, so closely associated with each other by common descent, language, or history as to form a distinct race or people'.[7] The cultural element is captured here by the commonality of descent, language, and history.

Of course, longstanding histories and traditions are part of many nations. Proof of this is that people can trace their language and history for hundreds, sometimes thousands of years. Still, nowhere in the world did or do nations exist as a fully common and coherent entity from the get-go. If we take the United Kingdom as an example, home to the *OED*, the British consist of English, Scots, Welsh, and Irish people. If they share a history, it is a history of wars fought against one another for a considerable part of it. Furthermore, these peoples in turn find their origins in the Celts, Anglo-Saxons (who hailed from continental Europe), Vikings (Danish and Norwegian), French Normans, and since the end of the colonial empire, many others.

In contrast to this impressive diversity, the notion of nation is propelled by the fiction that, as of old, people naturally and commonly belong to the places they are born and live in. Nation is derived from Latin *nasci*, 'to be born'. The idea is, firstly, that people are marked or defined by their descendants and the soil on which they were born. Secondly, somewhere in the past a nation was born, in the shape of a collective self, that started to develop itself in the course of time. Yet despite the natural-sounding term 'developed', it in fact requires a lot of maintenance to make a nation persist. For this maintenance, culture is key. A nation needs cultivation; it depends on culture, otherwise it loses its reason to exist.[8]

Whereas some nations claim to be very old (with or without good reason), others simply cannot boast of such ancestry, and it is at this point that the element of cultivation is granted another aura. Due to the rapid development of colonialism from the nineteenth century onwards, there are vast regions, even whole continents that have been divided by a few colonial powers. The artificial nation-states they constructed either dispersed peoples with their

7   *Oxford English Dictionary*, s.v. 'Nation'.
8   Leerssen, 'Nationalism and the Cultivation of Culture'.

cultures into different nation-states (like the Kurds, who live in Turkey, Syria, Iraq, and Iran) or merged different peoples and cultures within the border of one nation-state, as is the case in almost all of the Middle East and Africa. The result was the inevitable potential for civil war, a potential that did materialize in many of the newly constructed nation-states. Moreover, many of the European countries that became nation-states developed a so-called identity politics, which led to the exclusion or destruction of people who were not part of the proclaimed nation or culture. The partly successful attempt to destroy European Judaism is one horrific example; the colonial destruction of indigenous cultures and peoples on a global scale is another one.

History proves that it is possible for different cultures to coexist productively and peacefully within a state. India is a good case in point, counting more than 2000 different ethnic groups and 23 official languages. At the same time, India's case also illustrates the violent consequences of exclusion at other moments in history. If different cultures coexist peacefully within a given state, this invites the question of how political unity relates to cultural difference. It may be clear that difference cannot be a matter of homogeneity. To the contrary: the political entity that is able to keep this diversity intact can be the *state* as a polity with its many different citizens and groups, who become legal subjects due to the recognition of the state.

The *nation*, as a cultural and quasi-natural entity, does not coincide with the state, though clearly nation and state can, and have been conjoined. A third form of organisation in this context is *religion,* as an institution with its followers who share the belief in the possibility of transcendence as a spiritual community. If the three forms of organisation are fused, for instance, when a nation-state defines itself as a Hindu nation-state, this is a matter of identity politics, which is always a dangerous form of politics for those who are not considered to be part of the identity.

For instance, 14% of India's populace is Muslim at the moment. This may sound like a small number, but it still includes around 190 million people. Are they not to be given the feeling that they belong in India; and if not, what awaits them? These questions were not answered, but a clear signal was sent on 5 August 2019, when the presiding prime minister of India, Narendra Modi, removed the status of statehood of the only province in India with a majority of Muslims: Jammu and Kashmir. Then, exactly a year later, he took the time to ritually lay the cornerstone for a Hindu temple at Ayodhya. This is a temple that is being built on the ruins of a sixteenth-century mosque called Babri Masjid. The mosque did not turn into a ruin all by itself: it was destroyed by Hindu extremists in 1992 who believed it stood on the birthplace of the Hindu god Rama. Thousands have already died in the battles surrounding the site, all in the name of the fusion between state, nation, culture, and religion.

We started this section with the national anthem of India, perhaps the most populous country in the world. How many of the readers of this book will have recognized it? In case the Indian anthem is unfamiliar to readers, it is of interest to ask which national anthems they can hum. The answer to this question says a lot about their cultural background, training, and inclinations, but also says a lot about global hegemonies. If readers can hum the Indian anthem, they might know that its text was written by the famous Indian poet Rabindranath Tagore and that the Indian National Congress in Kolkata made it its decisive text on 27 December 1911. It only became India's national anthem in 1950. This thousands-year-old civilization, as claimed by Hindu nationalists, has a rather strikingly young national text and tune then.

In terms of text, the Japanese national anthem is the oldest national anthem, dating from the eighth century. Its melody, however, is from 1880, arranged by a German musician. The Dutch national anthem comes second, composed in the sixteenth century on the basis of a French victory song. The melody and text served as propaganda for William of Orange, who is considered to be the 'father of the fatherland' by the Dutch, but was declared or considered a terrorist by the Spanish king Philip II. The propaganda song defending William became the Netherlands' national anthem in 1932, though it now seems as if it has been the Dutch national anthem since the sixteenth century. In terms of melody, the Polish national anthem may be the oldest, dating from somewhere between the tenth and thirteenth century. Yet its text is from 1797, when it became a battle song; only in 1927 it became the national anthem. And as the second oldest national anthem makes clear: there are no pure origins to a culture, or a nation. For instance, the very same French melody of what is now the Dutch national anthem was also used in 1577 for a song about sex workers lamenting the fact that the Spanish troops had been chased out as a result of which they had to give up their profitable work.[9]

The nation-state is not the only collective realm that relates to the realm of culture. The term 'realm' indicates a certain space of agency that is rule-bound, in one way or another. If culture is a form-of-life, this connotes a specific *lifeworld*, hence a world different from others, which follows specific rules. This will be key to the next chapter, which draws a distinction between politics and the political.

9   Camerata Trajectina, 'Hoe die Spaanse hoeren komen klagen'.

3. Culture and the Political: A Multiplicity of Worlds

3.1. What is the connection between culture and world?

My friend came to me

With sadness in his eyes

He told me that he wanted help

Before his country dies

Although I couldn't feel the pain

I knew I had to try

Now I'm asking all of you

To help us save some lives

Bangladesh, Bangladesh

Where so many people are dying fast

And it sure looks like a mess

I've never seen such distress

'Bangla Desh' by George Harrison (1971)[1]

In the previous chapter we asked: in what sense is culture a matter of politics and how is culture used by politics? We focused especially on one of the most dominant ways in which culture was used by politics in the context of nation-states since the nineteenth century. In this context we considered how politics is about the ways in which the distribution of power can be used for certain purposes. Now we look at the ways in which a concept that is related to politics concerns the principal choice between different *worlds*. This concept is 'the political'. The term will be unpacked below, because when we talk about worlds, it is of scholarly importance to first distinguish between terms that are often used interchangeably, even if they mean different things: next to 'world', there are 'planet', 'earth', and 'globe'.

The term 'planet' denotes a celestial body in space. For instance, the earth is a planet with next-door neighbours Venus and Mars. 'Planet' etymologically means 'wanderer'. Astronomers noted early on that most stars have a fixed place in the sky, whilst certain isolated ones, planets, seemingly follow

---

1   Harrison, 'Bangla Desh'.

their own path through the night skies. Seen from one of the other planets, then, the planet 'Earth' never has one fixed position in the sky.

Encountered from out of space, the qualifier 'Earth' seems counterintuitive for a planet that consists mainly of water. Apparently, the term 'earth' is a description that defines the whole on the basis of a part, specifically the part from which one language-using species originates. The term 'earth' may also connote the difference between the everyday world of humans and the heavens, the domain of the gods. Earth, in that case, connotes the realm of the beings that are born, live, and die. As such, the term 'earth' is deeply cultural, precisely because it connotes the distribution of life and death (cf. Chapter 1).

The term 'globe' indicates something else, again, namely first and foremost a form with one solid, polished, and round shape. Due to the connection between 'globe' and 'globalization', Gayatri Chakravorty Spivak objected to this term precisely because it suggested that globalization is one solid, polished process that involves everyone equally. Spivak's argument was that it affects people very differently, unequally, and disparately, which is why she introduced the concept of *planetarity*.

Auritro Majumder, professor of English and cultural theory, summarizes the conceptual and political backbone of Spivak's work as follows:

> Spivak sees the term 'global' as produced by the convergence of multinational finance, media, and information technology. These are symptomatic of capital's tendency to homogenize and assimilate. 'Globalization,' Spivak says, 'is the imposition of the same system of exchange everywhere.' Unlike much of contemporary cultural theory, Spivak does not valorize globalization as a positive outcome whereby the sweeping tides of cultural exchange transform peripheral subjects into cosmopolitan global citizens. Globalization, or so the celebratory version of it goes, is supposedly an epistemic break from the past, freeing its subjects from their narrow prejudices and provincial affiliations toward new, decentered and even nonhuman horizons. Spivak's assessment is far more sober: 'in the gridwork of electronic capital, we achieve that abstract ball covered in latitudes and longitudes [...] now drawn by the requirements of Geographical Information Systems,' is how she links the capitalist production of the globe.[2]

The 'abstract ball' mentioned is the globe. Spivak argues that the reality of all sorts of processes feeding into the current situation is better denoted by

---

2   Majumder, 'Gayatri Spivak', 17. Quotations are from Spivak's *Death of a Discipline*, 72-73.

the term *planetarity*, which as a concept is capable of indicating that the collectives of human beings inhabit one wandering entity, a celestial body they share. However, this is also an entity that consists of a bricolage of different fragments and many inequalities. The planet does not show one polished or coherent surface, but a collection of parts, linked or separated, differently coloured and so forth. With respect to this, Spivak preferred the concept in order to emphasize the differences between people; differences that should be acknowledged, respected, criticized, addressed, or promoted. She even followed a decolonial agenda by saying: 'the planetarity of which I have been speaking [...] is perhaps best imagined from the pre-capitalist cultures of the planet'.[3] This statement implies that the current state of affairs is not a given but came to be orchestrated in asymmetrical ways, and always, or still, contains the potential of other worlds. Another term that was used to indicate that there is not one totality – even though there is always a power that is trying to suggest this – is *alterity*. This concept indicates that there are dynamics of diverse, ignored, but nevertheless autonomous entities that embody an alternative.[4]

If Spivak had used the concept 'world', this would have implied something else again. 'World' is derived from the fusion between 'wer'- (the same *wer*- as in *were*wolf: man-wolf) and -'alt', the first meaning mankind, and the second denoting a period in time. Thus, *world* indicates the situation of a species in time-space. This is why one can speak of several coexisting worlds, perhaps even many within a given universe. Such worlds can, but need not be, materially real. Many readers will have played the game *World of Warcraft*; fantasy in general presents people with a multiplicity of worlds, as does fiction. Yet there is also a multiplicity of materially real worlds. The world of ants is a world different from that of cats, and the world of cats is different from those of bacteria or human beings. Likewise, although most cultures are comparable and can interact, they can also be considered per se as connoting a separate world. Consequently, one would have to consider the possibility of not just one world, but of the simultaneous coexistence of a multiplicity of worlds. Worlds can split, that is, and multiply through splitting.

A separation of worlds was described by the American legal scholar Robert Cover (1943-1986) as a matter of *mitosis*. Mitosis is a biological term that denotes the splitting of one cell into two. It is this splitting on which all life depends. Culturally, politically, or legally speaking, it indicates a 'splitting of normative worlds' that is caused, according to Cover, by two

---

3   Spivak, *Death of a Discipline*, 101; for more on the 'decolonial', see Chapter 8.
4   On alterity, see for instance, Dussel, *Ethics of Liberation*. It was originally published in 1998.

opposing powers in any given society.[5] On the one hand, there is the state: a political entity that allows different people to live their own lives together, peacefully, in diversity. On the other hand, these peoples may form distinct, separate, homogenous, not compromise-oriented, and self-regulating communities. Cover defined the state as an 'imperial community' and the bottom-up communities as 'paideic communities'. The term *paideic* refers to the classical Greek and Roman term *paideia*, which describes the raising and training of young people to become citizens. Paideic communities, then, are communities that teach themselves how to live in a meaningful world: 'an integrated world of obligation and reality from which the rest of the world is perceived'.[6] They may not live together with others on the same basis, because they live according to a 'normative mitosis': a splitting of worlds on the basis of different or disparate norms.[7]

This split is analogous to what political theorist Chantal Mouffe defined as the pivot of 'the political': antagonism.[8] Politics, in her analysis, involves the relentless, never fully resolved struggle, or *agonism*, between different parties to stay together within a political body even though they disagree. The 'political' connotes that parties have interests which are ultimately incompatible. As long as these incompatibilities are made bearable by compromise, some form of unity may persist. Once incompatible interests are felt to be unbearable, this will probably lead to a division. Antagonism in such a case indicates that parties stand opposite to one another, as opponents.

One can consider the separation or partition of India and Pakistan in 1947, which until then had existed as one political realm under English rule, as a matter of political mitosis – a splitting that created two different nation-states and two different cultural worlds, one predominantly Muslim, one predominantly Hindu. Moreover, the Muslim one was divided into West and East Pakistan, the latter better known as Bengal – the biggest opium producer in the world under English rule. After partition, East Pakistan was the most densely populated area in the world. In 1971, it was also subject to another mitosis when a violent civil war between West and East Pakistan – with interventions by the Indian army – led to the independence of what is now called Bangladesh.

According to Cover, the world embodied in any paideic community is bound by a shared system of norms, a *nomos*, and a shared *narrative* that

---

5   Cover, 'Nomos and Narrative'. The article was originally published in 1983.
6   Ibid., 128.
7   Ibid., 128.
8   Mouffe, *On the Political*.

defines such a collective in its journey through space and time. The same holds for nation-states that almost exclusively define their beginnings from myths of origin (cf. Chapter 2): foundational narratives that propel their histories and contain sets of norms. Myth is a specific form of narrative that is especially suitable to explain the unexplainable origin of things.

Whereas narratives can be more or less convincing due to their logico-chronological ordering of things, myths emphasize the origin of things; they are a matter of belief. Hindu nationalists, for instance, cling to the myth that India has been a Hindu nation for thousands of years, with its very own beginning. The myth serves to express this beginning, whereas it also veils, by means of its narrative construction, that there is no such thing. On the basis of this double function of myth, some can claim India to be a homogenous nation-state: a state, with originally shared norms, that has the right to exclude others. This myth also has normative consequences, for instance, when it is said that one is not made a Hindu but born a Hindu. Whereas historical narratives are always characterized by contingency – a matter of the coincidental coming together of different elements – myths tend to conflate past, present, and future as if the three are one in terms of origin and destination.

Still, a study by the London-based sociologist and human rights scholar Chetan Bhatt, entitled *Hindu Nationalism: Origins, Ideologies and Modern Myths* (2001), argued that such myths are not a natural, original given at all. Most of them were constructed in conjunction with, and very much in service of, the construction of nation-states in the course of the eighteenth and nineteenth centuries. Their aim was to give the artificial construction of the nation-state a quasi-organic, primordial origin.

We started this chapter with a song by Beatles member George Harrison. Harrison and the Indian-Bengali composer and sitar player Ravi Shankar had organized two benefit concerts to collect money to alleviate the abysmal circumstances that determined the lives of the people of Bangladesh during the war of independence. The two concerts took place on the very same day, 1 August 1971, in Madison Square Garden in New York City. During the evening concert, when Ravi Shankar's crew had merely been tuning the instruments, the audience broke out in applause. Shankar replied: 'If you appreciate the tuning so much, I hope you will enjoy the playing more.'[9] The concert is an example of how culture can be used to make money, which will be the topic of Chapter 4. The misrecognition

9   NPR, 'Ravi Shankar'.

of what Shankar and his team were doing is the core of the next part of this chapter. Shankar's tuning of the sitar was not recognized as such by people who apparently lived in their own world, and were not able to distinguish the different forms of music operative in another one. It is just one index to the multiplicity of worlds simultaneously operative in relation to culture.

3.2.   How does culture connote a multiplicity of worlds?

> The hills are alive with the sound of music
> With songs they have sung for a thousand years
> The hills fill my heart with the sound of music
> My heart wants to sing every song it hears
> My heart wants to beat like the wings of the birds
> That rise from the lake to the trees
> My heart wants to sigh like a chime that flies
> From a church on a breeze
> To laugh like a brook when it trips and falls over
> Stones on its way
> To sing through the night like a lark who is learning to pray

'The Sound of Music' by Julie Andrews (1965)[10]

The issue central to this part of Chapter 3 is how cultures can connote worlds that exist simultaneously. If one planet can host many worlds, or a multiplicity of worlds, this entails implications for how they intersect, mingle, exist next to one another and are somehow separate at the same time. Arundhati Roy's novel *The God of Small Things*, from 1997, will be our guide in explaining how this may work. Central to *The God of Small Things* is an illicit love between a middle- or upper-class woman named Ammu, and a man called Velutha who belongs to a group of people that exists beneath the lowest caste of labourers.

The Indian caste system was given different names throughout history, but the Portuguese term 'casta' became the most well-known during colonialism, the period during which the Indian caste system was intensified and strengthened for the purposes of the British. In his study of the historical and present status of the caste system, *Castes of Mind: Colonialism and the*

---

10   Andrews, 'The Sound of Music'.

Making of Modern India (2001), the anthropologist and historian Nicholas B. Dirks noticed that:

> Caste may no longer convey a sense of community that confers civilizational identity to the Indian subcontinent, but it is still the primary form of local identity and, in certain contexts, from Dalits to Brahmans, translates the local into recognizable subcontinental idioms of association far more powerful than any other single category of community.[11]

Dirks contends that, while castes marked the entire social order of Indian civilization in the past and the general force of the system may have lost some of its impact, caste still defines communities and the borders between them on a local scale, and powerfully so. Here, the people that are even considered to be less than the lowest caste (connoted by the term 'outcasts') are called Dalits, derived from 'Dal', meaning 'broken', 'banned', or 'unjust'. People from this group have also been given the derogatory name 'untouchables'. Dalit can be considered a political concept in so far as it defines a positive redefinition of this status. Communities of Dalits make up 16% of the Indian populace. Since the Indian populace numbered 1.4 billion people in 2020, this means that there are around 224 million Dalits.

Although the Indian government has established programmes for the improvement of the status of Dalits for a couple of decades, they are not yet fully accepted citizens. Roy's novel shows as much, since the love affair between a woman from a higher caste and a person who belongs to a group lower than the lowest caste seems impossible; illicit. It will cost Velutha his life. If we consider a multiplicity of cultural worlds, India's caste system is a textbook example. Note that the border between the two worlds of castes is not closed, as the love between Ammu and Velutha illustrates. However, it is asymmetrically porous or unequally crossable for either party. Untouchables are needed in the world of higher castes to do the cleaning, take care of the garden, and take out the garbage, but a higher-class person will never enter the world of Dalits – nor should she enter into a relationship with one of them.

The novel also takes the readers to the world of Ammu's two children, boy and girl twins named Estha and Rahel. They live in their own world, the world of children. It is in part a fantasy world, marked by its own secrets, and a world that can intersect with both the world of their mother and her lover's, although the children have no knowledge of their love. Central to their own universe is an abandoned house described as 'the history

11   Dirks, *Castes of Mind*, 7.

house', since it belonged to a colonial Englishman who 'had gone native'. The latter phrase connotes yet another multiplicity of worlds. Colonials either stuck to their own universe, or they transgressed to the world of the so-called 'others' (on which more in Chapter 8) as a result of which they were considered to be traitors by one side and strangers by the other. The colonial era also connotes another multiplicity that emphasizes the time aspect of time-space. One clear example is that the family in the novel consists of Syrian Christians, or St. Thomas Christians, a group of Indian believers that traces its history to the preaching of St. Thomas in the first century. They are a notable exception in a predominantly Hindu nation.

Evidently, the fact that we are focusing on a novel, highlights that there is also the difference between the world of daily reality and that of fiction. Yet fiction is also part of everyday reality in that it caters to the existence of other worlds. One prominent event in the novel, for instance, is the protagonists' visit to the musical *The Sound of Music* from 1965. This movie is set in Austria during the period of the Nazi annexation of the country in the 1930s. It is a Hollywood movie with an all-white cast; the English actress Julie Andrews plays the protagonist. It is a fine product of the culture industry (which will be elaborated in the next chapter). The movie presents its own world, the world of the story set in Austria, but also demonstrates the power of the former colonial British Empire through the protagonist. Moreover, as a Hollywood movie from the 1960s, it is also a product of US cultural hegemony. Meanwhile, in the novel, it is watched by an all-Indian audience, including different castes, different religions, and different generations; all of them having their own interpretation of the movie.

As may have become clear, a multiplicity of worlds does not mean that all these worlds are closed-off entities merely occurring next to one another. They exist simultaneously, they will frame one another, intermingle, but can also remain unaware of each other. One question raised in a song by the American singer-songwriter Paul Simon, entitled 'Questions for the Angels', is: 'If every human on the planet / and all the buildings on it / should disappear / would a zebra grazing in the African savanna / care enough to shed one zebra tear?'[12] Likewise, one could ask how many tears human beings have shed over the destruction of the lifeworld of zebras, or when they destroy an ant's nest, a nest of wasps, a fly, or four-fifths of life on this planet. Culturally speaking, some questions closer to home are how many human beings shed a tear when millions of so-called others are starving from hunger. Of course, many will shed a tear, but do they feel their own lifeworld to be part of that other, dying world; or would they rather keep the two apart?

12   Simon, 'Questions for the Angels'.

In the context of worlds, a much used and much-debated term nowadays is 'intersectionality'. It was coined by the legal scholar Kimberlé Crenshaw, in a paper from 1989 entitled 'Demarginalizing the Intersection of Race and Sex'.[13] Crenshaw was collaborating with others in developing a critical race theory that would oppose a common fantasy underpinning the rule of law, which held that 'once the irrational distortions of bias were removed, the underlying legal and socioeconomic order would revert to a neutral, benign state of impersonally apportioned justice'.[14] Crenshaw's argument postulated that if a complex case was brought to court, it happened in conjunction with the illusion that such a court would be capable of including the issue of race professionally and judge its connection to other aspects, say aspects of gender, labour, and other forms of hierarchy and inequality. Yet both the strength and the weakness of law is that it will always, almost anatomically, separate things. Courts will deal with entities as long as they fall under a certain rule, one that needs to be strict, otherwise there is a 'mix up'. In this specific case, African-American women had filed charges against their employer on the charge of discrimination. The judge thought otherwise, given that the court could decide on either gender, race, or age, but not on the intrinsic combination of these factors.

Crenshaw's analysis was spot on in showing that for the law, the world of low-paid and low-educated African-American women is another one than that of high-paid, highly educated white women. And the urgency of her concept is not something of the past, as her TED talk in October 2016 made clear.[15] Alongside its legal origin, the term 'intersectionality' started to travel and has become a common concept in the social sciences and humanities. Here, many tend to acknowledge the issue of friction between worlds, whilst struggling with the question of how to combine a multiplicity of worlds without extinguishing individual and particular autonomies.

We started this chapter with the opening song of *The Sound of Music*. Prior to becoming a movie, the musical was a Broadway hit from 1959 onwards, written by composer Richard Rodgers and lyricist and dramatist Oscar Hammerstein II. Rodger's family name had been Rogazinsky; he was the child of German Jews. His father had judged it wise to assimilate into American culture, softening the borders between worlds by adopting an Americanized name.

---

13   Crenshaw, 'Demarginalizing the Intersection of Race and Sex'.
14   Coaston, 'The Intersectionality Wars'.
15   Crenshaw and Dobson, *The Urgency of Intersectionality.*

As for a more conflicting mixture of worlds, one of the children in Roy's novel, *The God of Small Things*, the boy, Estha, annoys the audience because he is singing along; he is ordered to leave. He continues singing the song outside the cinema hall, finishing with the line: 'How do you keep a moon-beam in your hand?' As a brutal counterpart to this poetic image, Estha is then addressed by the Orangedrink Lemondrink Man, who gives him a soda but also ends up sexually abusing the little boy. It is both a confrontation between, and a conflation of the world of the movie characters, who are so clean they all seem to come out of a long soak in a bath, and a consumer culture that produces a world of beautiful illusions and hides the violence to which these are connected. For a moment Estha gets lost in another world. It is a world, moreover, that in contemporary reality has turned into a global black market for horrendous abuses due to the widely accessible internet.

With consumer culture another kind of power is involved than the political one: the power of the market. Above we considered distributions of power when looking at the relations between culture and politics and the political, firstly, defined by the notion of the nation-state and, secondly, by the world. Meanwhile, no attention was paid to another kind of distribution, of not just goods and things but also possibilities. In the distribution of all sorts of power and possibilities two concepts are pivotal that were distinguished by the seventeenth-century philosopher Benedict de Spinoza (1632-1677) as *potestas* and *potentia*.[16] Both connote a form of power. *Potestas* concerns a power from above, executed by authorities – or markets. *Potentia* indicates the potential residing in everything that exists – and this might also include markets.

In the context of culture, we consider the distribution of potentiality and power as follows: culture is an evolutionary phenomenon that is a formative and empowering *technique* for humans. This technique is in no one's hands, but is in itself a form of subjection that can be (and in many instances *is*) used by other powers, as a matter of *potestas*. Culture also embodies peoples' and animals' *potentiality*: i.e. it is an empowering template for the capacity and ability to not just live but to shape and *form* one's life.

We will look at the relations between cultures and economies and different kinds of economies in the next two chapters. Central to these chapters are no-tions of value, and how these are not just a matter of money but also of affect. In relation to value, we will ask how the two, culture and economy, connect by means of two other types of collective bodies: society and civilization.

---

16 Spinoza developed his thoughts in more than a decade, between 1661 and 1675. They were only published in 1677 as *Ethica* or *Ethics* after his death. For an introduction, see Lloyd, *Routledge Philosophy Guidebook*.

4. Culture and Economies: Society

4.1. Society: How is value determined economically and culturally?

> We were all wounded at Wounded Knee
> You and me
> We were all wounded at Wounded Knee
> You and me
> In the name of manifest destiny
> You and me you and me you and me.
>
> They made us many promises
> But always broke their word
> They penned us in like buffalo
> Drove us like a herd
> And finally on the reservation
> We were going for our preservation
> We were all wiped out by the Seventh Calvary
> You and me you and me.

'We Were All Wounded at Wounded Knee' by Redbone (1972)[1]

This chapter and the next look at the relation between culture and economies and consider in what senses culture may define forms of *value*. In Chapter 4 this concerns economic value, while Chapter 5 concentrates on how cultures may affectively determine economic models and how culture itself can become a commodity. The two chapters consider culture and economies respectively in relation to society and to civilization.

Can the same economic system operate in different cultures? This is the basic question that helps us to explore the force field between culture and economy. One can argue, for instance, that the current form of capitalism determines all national and international markets. But does it function exactly the same way in China, in Argentina, in Belgium, in Ethiopia, in New Zealand, in Bahrain, or in Canada? Well, it does and does not. Perhaps one of the advantages of capitalism is that it is culturally flexible and adapts itself

---

1   Redbone, 'We Were All Wounded at Wounded Knee'.

quickly.[2] We can also reverse the issue. The question: can the same economic system operate in different cultures? then becomes: are specific forms of economy culturally determined? The answer to both questions will depend strongly on how economic values are determined by cultural values, or vice versa. Perhaps, the questions will sound strange to economists. They might wonder what economy has to do with culture in the first place. Economy is a separate domain of life to them, in which people exchange goods on the basis of their interests and distribute them in order to be able to live.

Anthropologist David Graeber (1961-2020) shed light on the relations between culture and economies. He spent years on studying the relation between the two and summarized the results in a study entitled *Debt: The First 5,000 Years* (2011). The major claim in this study is that people are always indebted to one another, and the forms this indebtedness takes are culturally determined. Historically, indebtedness is defined informally in most economies and cannot be measured with exactitude. Nevertheless, it is pivotal to any form of communal life. For instance, it is simply impossible to build a house entirely on your own: people need others to help them. Besides needing loads of equipment, they will have to know how to build a house. Knowledge that others will have provided is also a form of indebtedness. In this respect, informal economies are radically different from societies in which money rules all affairs. In such societies debt has turned into a calculable matter of mathematical rigor.

The Dutch Central Bureau of Statistics noticed rising student debt, for instance, in the last two decades. In less than ten years the number of students with a debt has almost doubled, and so has the average amount of debt. In the Netherlands, students now have debt of €19.3 billion, collectively, which comes down to an average debt of roughly €13,800 for 1.4 million people.[3] In the case of the United States of America, medicine or law students have undergone the same. The average has almost doubled since 2000, with average debts of $246,000 (medicine) and $145,500 (law). These averages imply that some students enter their adult lives and careers towing an anchor of debt of over $300,000.[4]

The opposite of indebtedness is giftedness. Most economies in history, however culturally diverse, have functioned on the basis of gifts.

2   This issue was addressed by scholars who investigated cultural interactions from a business perspective, such as organizational psychologist Geert Hofstede and his son, Gert Jan Hofstede, or Professor of Organizational Behaviour Erin Meyer. We will return to their work in Chapter 9 when dealing with the issues of translation and transaction.

3   CBS, 'Studenten lenen vaker en meer'.

4   McFarland, 'Trends in Graduate Student Loan Debt'.

The procedure of gifting was studied by the French ethnologist Marcel Mauss (1872-1950) in *Essai sur le don: Forme et raison de l'échange dans les sociétés archaïques* (1924) – or *The Gift: The Form and Reason for Exchange in Archaic Societies* (1954). The subtitle suggests that any act of gifting carries a particular motivation and form. Nowadays gifts are mostly used to smooth social or cultural relations – not a minor endeavour, but also not central to cultural or economic exchange. Compared to previous societies, however, the gift has become a marginal phenomenon. In the current state of affairs, the marginality of the gift is the counterpart to efficiency and calculation in a consumer culture that is deeply obsessed with the self-interest of individuals.

The classic image of the economic individual proposed by Adam Smith (1723-1790) is that the economic being is a rational one if it participates in the market. In the opinion of Karl Marx (1818-1883), the capitalist economic subject is greedy and exploitative. Yet according to the feminist social geographer J.K. Gibson-Graham – a scholarly penname of Julie Graham (1945-2000) and Katherine Gibson – individual subjects as such do not exist. Instead, there is always a network of related subjects, with different economies occurring simultaneously. It is this mixture that implies culture and affective relations.

More generally, the realization that economic beings are not rational individuals led to a shift in the analysis. As economist Raquel Fernández noted in the abstract of her article 'Culture and Economics':

> Modern neoclassical economics has, until recently, ignored the potential role of culture in explaining variation in economic outcomes, largely because of the difficulty in rigorously separating the effects of culture from those of institutions and traditional economic variables.[5]

Apparently, the difficulty is to disentangle the cultural from the economic, which does not mean that it is impossible. The solution lies not in considering the two as separate domains, but as two aspects of a given *society*.

Society is derived from *societatem*, meaning 'fellowship, association, alliance, union, community', which in turn is connected to *socius*, 'companion, ally'. In all these cases people meet on the basis of shared interests and abilities, which, first and foremost, holds a promise and allows them to exchange and distribute things. In principle, people from different cultures can be fellows, allies, or companions. This is what defines cultural interaction. Many markets throughout history testify to such collaboration. The

5   Fernández, 'Culture and Economics'.

ways in which such interactions take place even include a cultural aspect in and of itself. The markets of Rome are different from those of Beijing, which again differ from the markets in the African city of Benin, just as the London financial centre is unlike the markets in Frankfurt or Shanghai.

By considering both culture and economy as aspects of a society, one can trace their interaction on the basis of what people value, and how this determines what they exchange and distribute. Cultures are driven by values, as are the commonly held standards of what is acceptable or unacceptable, important or unimportant, right or wrong, workable or unworkable, cherished or detested, etc. Such cultural value may be *analogous* to the notion of economic value, but the two are not the *same*. Economic value is commonly defined as 'the maximum amount of money a specific actor is willing and able to pay for the good or service'.[6] It is something other than price, then, or even market value. If you are no fan of teddy bears, for instance, you would purchase one for a market value of, let's say, €8. However, the price depends immensely on the current level of inflation. In the case of hyperinflation, the price could explode to €8000 within months. Moreover, if you are a collector of teddy bears, and are missing this one item in your collection, you might go well beyond the market value. A teddy bear of €8 market value could then yield €18000.

Teddy bears may also be a good example of how value is determined culturally, not only in the context of a commercial, industrialized market of stuffed animals, but also a US-dominated one. The teddy bear was named after the 26th president of the United States, Theodore (Teddy) Roosevelt (1858-1919), whose hobby it was to hunt bears. Hence, the teddy bear is historically valued by way of a culture that idolized the 'manly' sport of hunting. Nowadays, it is at the core of a consumer culture that either considers animals to be isolated pieces of meat or values them as objects for coddling.

Value determines not only distribution. As anthropologist David Graeber argued, what people deem to be valuable or not, is at the heart of politics.[7] Now, if value lies at the core of both politics and economic distribution, what could its intrinsic cultural parameters be? One telling example from 20202 is that Uluru, a sandstone formation in Australia also known as Ayers Rock, stopped being a mountain available to be climbed by tourists because aboriginals did not accept it as an object of distribution. Being a holy mountain, it was beyond distribution and was not to be shared. To many Westerners, such a prohibition may strike one as strange. Why wouldn't

6   Wikipedia, 'Value (economics)'.
7   Graeber, *Toward an Anthropological Theory of Value*.

tourists be allowed to climb such a picturesque and intriguing mountain? However, they may tend to forget that their own private property is also sacrosanct. Once they have bought a house, it is no longer part of the realm of distribution, and no one is allowed to interfere with it without the owner's consent. After all, many homeowners were mightily upset in the summer of 2018 when *Pokémon Go* was a hit and players entered private properties where virtual animals were located.

One difference between the holy mountain and a private property is that the first cannot be bought or exchanged, but this does not mean that the two are separate. Most of the time, there is a coincidence of political, economic, and cultural values that have *interest* as their pivot, in all the different meanings and connotations of the term 'interest' – ranging from having a financial stake in things to being interested in something, and from investments to commitments.

In their relation to value, forms of exchange that are not necessarily economic can be considered as a paradigm of cultural interaction. For instance, Graeber studied the use and exchange of strings or belts of wampum (beads made from conches or scallop shells) by Native Americans. In his studies, Graeber found that the wampum had great spiritual power for the Iroquois, even in the sense that they could bring back the dead.[8] Culturally, these artefacts were highly valued without their containing any economic value. They were reappropriated economically and culturally, however, once Europeans took note of them. According to them, wampum was a form of currency by means of which things could be exchanged. As Graeber noted:

> English and Dutch colonists apparently found it a relatively simple matter to force [the Narragansetts and Pequots] to mass-produce the wampum beads, stringing them together in belts of pure white or pure purple and setting fixed rates of exchange with the Indians of the interior; so many fathoms of wampum for such and such a pelt.[9]

In terms of value, the relation between culture and economy was different then for Native Americans and the newly arrived colonizers who had started to make the new lands theirs. For the former, the wampum was part of a gift culture. The colonizers considered wampum to be fit for trade and as a means to make an easy profit, because the cost of their production was so minimal.

8   Ibid.
9   Graeber quoted in Tweedy, 'From Beads to Bounty'.

We began this chapter with a song from 1973 by the band Redbone, 'We Were All Wounded at Wounded Knee'. This song topped the charts in many European countries, but not in the United States. Even worse, the song was banned from radio stations and boycotted by the music industry. There were both political and cultural explanations for this, because the song is a reminder of a pivotal moment in the elimination of Native Americans: the bloodbath at Wounded Knee in South Dakota, on 29 December 1890, when Lakota people were ordered by a US Army patrol to return to their reservation. A struggle ensued and all the members of the community, including the women and children, were killed. In general, the elimination of Native American peoples did not only include entire cultures that were destroyed or marginalized, but also alternative forms of economic exchange and value distribution.

The second part of this chapter discusses a more recent, contemporary situation in which a society was violently restructured on the basis of both economic and cultural incentives.

4.2.   How are economies determined by culture and can culture be used economically?

El derecho de vivir
Poeta Ho Chi Minh
Que golpea de Vietnam
A toda la humanidad
Ningún cañón borrará
El surco de tu arrozal
El derecho de vivir en paz

'El derecho de vivir en paz' by Victor Jara (1971)[10]

The epigraph for this chapter is taken from a song by Chilean singer-songwriter Victor Jara (1932-1973). He was Chile's most popular and famous musician, singer, and guitar player at the time. In the coup d'état that took place on 11 September 1973 – notably, quite another 9/11 than the one from 2001 – the elected socialist president Salvador Allende (1908-1973) was killed and General Augusto Pinochet (1915-2006) was installed as the country's new leader. Jara was immediately captured, and like many other young intellectuals, brought to the football stadium of Santiago de Chile that functioned as

10   Jara, 'El derecho de vivir en paz'.

an impromptu concentration camp. He was identified, separated from the others, tortured, and killed. He was found eventually, with all ten fingers crushed and his body mutilated by 30 bullet holes.

Some people consider this coup d'état as merely a political matter, but it was in fact a turnover that led to a gigantic economic experiment once the newly installed president gave a free pass to followers of the Chicago School of Economics. This is what American business columnist James Flanigan had to say about Chile's case. According to Flanigan, the country's turnover had been a positive thing because it had changed things economically:

> In a sense, it all began in Chile. In the early 1970s, Chile was one of the first economies in the developing world to test such concepts as deregulation of industries, privatization of state companies, freeing of prices from government control, and opening of the home market to imports. [...] In 1981, Chile privatized its social-security system. [...] Many of those ideas [...] ultimately spread throughout Latin America and to the rest of the world. [...] They are behind the reformation of Eastern Europe and the states of the former Soviet Union today. [...] In some measure, Chilean economics are the prescription for bringing ailing Asian economies back to health [...] which demonstrates, once again, the awesome power of ideas.[11]

The so-called 'awesome powers of ideas' was much determined by the aforementioned Chicago School of Economics, Milton Friedman being one of its iconic figures. He, in turn, was closely associated with Ayn Rand-style capitalism. Who is she, and why is she of interest when studying the cultural determination of economies?

Ayn Rand, maiden name Alissa Zinovievna Rosenbaum, was born in St. Petersburg in 1905. She witnessed the Russian revolution and left communist Russia for New York in 1924 (she died in 1982). There she became a self-styled philosopher and author of influential novels such as *The Fountainhead* (1943) and *Atlas Shrugged* (1957). She also had a circle of students, or followers, like Alan Greenspan, who was head of the Federal Reserve System from 1987 to 2006, the heyday of neoliberalism. Furthermore, she inspired Nobel prize winner Milton Friedman, the key figure in the Chicago School of Economics. According to them, individualism and a radically free market were the pivots of any economic system. State regulation was the enemy.

In a set of essays called *The Virtue of Selfishness: A New Concept of Egoism*, Rand stated: 'The three cardinal values of the Objectivist ethics – the three

11   Flanigan, 'Pinochet Aside'.

values which, together, are the means to and the realization of one's ultimate value, one's own life – are: Reason, Purpose, Self-Esteem, with their three corresponding virtues: Rationality, Productivity, Pride."[12] All these concepts are deeply culturally coloured, yet they were defined as a matter of what Rand called 'Objectivist ethics', a phrase that suggests a universal and non-cultural status. Sure, to a contemporary Western mind, productivity may be a self-evident 'virtue'. There have been and there are cultures, however, in which inactivity is highly praised (an issue to which we will return in Chapter 7), or in which productivity should serve the well-being of the collective.

Ayn Rand could just have been one of the many authors occupying the literary landscape. Nevertheless, her vision on how societies should be organized had an ostentatious influence on American politics, especially the Republican Party, which was studied by Jennifer Burns in a biography entitled *Goddess of the Market: Ayn Rand and the American Right* (2009). Moreover, she had a circle of followers since the 1940s, ironically called 'The Collective', that included figures such as Alan Greenspan in the 1950s. During this decade, this circle of people would discuss the new novel of Ayn Rand, *Atlas Shrugged*, which is probably not that well known to an international audience, but that is of considerable importance in a US context. Where literary experts struggle to see its value, a general audience values it enormously. It is a relentless defence of capitalism and the self-interest that propels it.

According to Rand, those who defend solidarity and equality are either 'looters' or 'moochers'. The looters are those who propose taxes to distribute money more fairly, and the moochers are those who benefit from it. In her own words:

> Individualism regards man –every man– as an independent, sovereign entity who possesses an inalienable right to his own life, a right derived from his nature as a rational being. Individualism holds that a civilized society, or any form of association, cooperation or peaceful coexistence among men, can be achieved only on the basis of the recognition of individual rights – and that a group, as such, has no rights other than the individual rights of its members.[13]

It does not take a leap of faith to realize how these ideas only make sense on the basis of cultural presuppositions that promote individualism and have their origin in the United Kingdom and the United States. In many

---

12   Rand and Branden, *The Virtue of Selfishness*, 25.
13   Ibid., 25-26.

cultures, it is not the individual but the collective that is the most important building block of a civilized society. Moreover, the 'right to his own life' led Rand to postulate that the primary interest of individuals is to pursue their own interests, regardless of others. Yet in many cultures care for the other is a dominant quality. Nevertheless, since the 1950s, Rand's theories and novels came to inspire and support a movement that would result in the reconstructions of national and international economies on a global scale. All of these were advertised as 'rational', in order to hide the fact that they, too, were part of a distinct cultural presupposition.

Additionally, another shift was happening in this context. Culture, both capital and small c, came to be considered increasingly as a matter of exchange itself; as a commodity, that is. Culture sells. Or, since the middle of the nineteenth century, culture, both capital and small c, had become of interest as an industry. It led German philosophers Theodor Adorno (1903-1969) and Max Horkheimer (1895-1973) to define it as an entire and separate industry.[14] Their analysis proclaimed that this kind of industry dulled the masses and led them to accept situations of injustice, pacifying them by means of a form of art that prioritized consumption.

Whatever way we look at it, the last two centuries leave little doubt as to whether the economization of culture has taken place. It is a process that has only been intensified by the arrival of mass media and social media: everything has become part of some sort of market. Reversely, this has led to a culturalization of politics and economy. Partly, this is the case because everything has been included in a mediatized reality. Yet another form of culturalization was noticed by political theorist Wendy Brown. In her analysis, all sorts of conflicts, whether political, economic, social, colonial, or ecological, are being redefined by influential Western actors to become a matter of culture.

> The culturalization of politics analytically vanquishes political economy, states, history, and international and transnational relations. It eliminates colonialism, capital, caste or class stratification, and external political domination from accounts of political conflict or instability. In their stead, 'culture' is summoned to explain the motives and aspirations leading to certain conflicts.[15]

Brown's argument is that important actors consider Western societies not as culturally marked, but instead as 'objective' and living according to universal

14   Horkheimer and Adorno, 'The Culture Industry'.
15   Brown, *Regulating Aversion*, 20.

'civilizational standards' – the same rhetorical trick that Rand played. This allows them to use culture as a negative indicative. Playing the cultural card in this case means that others are so culturally marked that they can never be enlightened enough to embrace Western modes of economy and the market. We will return to this in the next chapter.

We introduced this part of Chapter 4 with a song written and composed by Victor Jara: 'The Right to Live in Peace'. The song regained fame during the Chilean protests against the country's massive inequalities in fall 2019, yet with a text that was different from the original 1971 version.[16] In the latter version, Jara was singing the praise of Ho-Chi Minh – the communist leader of North Vietnam at the time of in its war for independency and autonomy. The 'American War', as it is called in Vietnam, had started in 1955 and would only end in 1975. Jara's 1971 version can still be found on YouTube – and with hindsight, the close-up picture of his hands playing the guitar are a chilling foreboding of the torture that would kill him. The different song versions illustrate how the culture of the 1970s and the current cultural climate are markedly different. The new text, based on Jara's original song, is adjusted and smoothed in a call for a new social pact. The details of what that pact would be or what it would require are unclear. This does not mean that the desire for such change is not real. In the 2019 protests, the government responded with violence, positioning tanks on the streets and ordaining a curfew that demanded silence from its citizens. It led opera singer Ayleen Jovita Romero to look for culture during a protest. She sang 'The Right to Live in Peace' from her balcony at night and was rewarded with hails of support.[17] In general, both versions of the song testify to the fact that, in any protest, against whatever form of injustice, culture plays a pivotal role.

In the next chapter, we will zoom in more closely on interactions between culture and economies that are affectively charged, with a particular focus on what people define as 'civilized' – or not.

16   Grck7, *The Right to Live in Peace*.
17   *Scroll* staff. 'Watch: A Soprano in Chile'.

5.   Culture and Affective Economies: Civilization

Costume design for *Le sacre du printemps* by Igor Stravinsky (1913)[1]

5.1.   Civilization: How are cultural hierarchies always affectively charged?

Let us start this chapter with two simple questions: how do you like your coffee and when do you drink it? The answer to these questions involves matters of cultural background, or of a difference between generations. It may involve the dominance of a specific consumer culture, and it will connote subcultures, for example, when people only enjoy the coffee made

1   Dalbéra, *Lélue (Sacre du printemps, ballets russes)*.

from a specific type of bean by a specific café. Globally, an Italian coffee culture has come to govern the consumption of coffee as when people can choose between a cappuccino, latte, espresso, espresso macchiato, and so forth. Even if you order an Americano, this is an Italian term, which originally indicated a weak espresso (by adding hot water), making Italian espresso coffee resemble the filter coffee that Americans were used to. The preference for filter coffee may be part of an older generation that was not familiar with Italian coffee culture yet, but it is also culturally determined. Currently, filter coffee is considered to be more sophisticated by experts, for instance, and in Colombia – not a minor coffee country. Additionally, whereas people in some countries need coffee as a boost in the morning, in other cultures people may enjoy it throughout the day, or specific parts of the day may coincide with different kinds of coffee.

The way in which coffee is made may even connote hierarchies of value or civilization. The so-called Senseo coffee machine was developed in the Netherlands and became a national and international commercial success. Meanwhile, it has also become a popular target on Twitter. On this platform, the comments imply that people who drink Senseo coffee have inferior taste. Apparently, according to the critics, making coffee is considered to be an art not easily mastered by anyone. My father would certainly not have belonged to such masters. Born in 1921 as a farmer's son, he was used to coffee that was kept warm on the stove throughout the day and the leftovers of the previous day would be heated up the next morning – horror of horrors to coffee aficionados! The latter term is not Italian, by the way, but Spanish and helps to distinguish between commoners, so-called 'fans', and the more intellectual 'connoisseurs'.[2] An aficionado is passionate about something, which emphasizes that the issue under consideration is a matter of feelings, style, and, as such, hierarchy.

This simple example may serve to illustrate a much broader characteristic of how people interact culturally. They tend to hierarchize. The Ancient Greeks called people of other cultures 'barbarians'. Jews may call non-Jews goyim. 'Goy' originally means nothing other than a 'people' (cf. the English translation: 'gentiles', derived from the Latin *gens*), but the qualification 'people' easily shifts into something more negative like 'commoners', or 'the rabble'. Likewise, Muslims have a word for people who are not one of them: *kafir*, an Arabic term which refers to a person who is a nonbeliever or who rejects the tenets of Islam. Catholics called those who believed something else 'heretics' or 'Cathars' (a reference to a medieval non-Catholic Christian

---

2   One example is a website on 'Intelligentsia Coffee' that teaches people how to become an aficionado: Eagle Rock Café, 'How to Taste Coffee'.

movement). Colonizers called other peoples 'savages', 'primitives', and frequently compared them to animals – or children, the small barbarians. Time and again, distinctions are made on the basis of a hierarchy that depends on the conception that one's own people are civilized whereas others are not, or only to much lesser degrees.

In light of this, an uproar occurred during a meeting of the major world leaders in Germany on 8 July 2018. The leaders were discussing the European migration issue and considered whether it would be helpful if Europe did the same thing with Africa today as what the United States did after World War II with the Marshall Plan, which provided massive financial support for the reconstruction of Europe. Rejecting the idea, French president Macron expressed a view that was quoted in the French newspaper *Le Monde*: 'Plan Marshall était un plan de reconstruction, dans des pays qui avaient leurs équilibres, leurs frontières, leur stabilité. [...] Le défi de l'Afrique est différent, il est beaucoup plus profond, il est civilisationnel.'[3] That is: 'The Marshall plan was a reconstruction plan in countries that were more or less balanced, had their borders, their stability. [...] The African challenge is different, it is much more serious, it is a matter of civilization' (my translation). If Macron was really saying that a 'Marshall Plan' for Africa would not work because of a civilizational problem, this seemed to express a colonial attitude on the part of a former colonial power.

In order to provide more context, the French word *'civilisation'* can indicate three different things, following the *Larousse dictionnaire de français*:

> (1) The action of civilizing a region, a people, of perfectioning the material and cultural conditions in which a people lives – cf. the civilization of Gaul by the Romans. (2) The state of economic, social, political, cultural development that certain societies have achieved and which is considered to be an ideal that others aim to achieve; synonym: culture – opposite meaning: barbarity, savagery. (3) The collection of characteristics specific to the intellectual, artistic, moral, social and material life of a country or society – cf. the civilization of the Incas.[4]

---

3   Gwet, 'Pour la France'.
4   '1. Action de civiliser un pays, un peuple, de perfectionner les conditions matérielles et culturelles dans lesquelles vivent un peuple; *La civilization de la Gaule par les Romains*. 2. État de developpement économique, social, politique, culturel auquel sont parvenues certaines sociétés et qui est considèré comme un ideal à atteindre par les autres. Synonyme: Culture; Contraires: barbarie, sauvagerie. 3. Ensemble des caractères propres à la vie intellectuelle, artistique, morale, sociale et materièlle d'un pays ou d'une société; *La civilization des Incas*' (*Larousse dictionnaire de français*, 'civilisation n.f.').

The first meaning can be qualified as imperialistic or colonial. The second one indicates whether or not one can speak of a duly or admirably functioning civil society. The third meaning is equivalent to English 'culture', small c. Note, here, that the French word *culture* also has multiple meanings, then, for *Larousse* gives 'culture' as a synonym for civilized society, as the opposites of barbarity and savagery indicate. Culture means 'civilized' here, as a matter of culture with a capital C. What Macron said did not concern the third but probably the second meaning of 'civilized'. Nevertheless, it also carried the nasty implication that African culture needed to be civilized first and thereby it connoted the imperial and colonial meaning of 'civilization'.

The relation between civilization and economic interests was traced by the sociologists Émile Durkheim and Marcel Mauss (also author of *The Gift*; see previous chapter) in a study called 'Note on the Notion of Civilization'.[5] Their characteristics of the term 'civilization' were defined by the Swedish-American sociologist Richard Swedberg as follows.[6] First of all, societies can be controlled politically, whereas civilizations cannot; they exceed societies. This is in accordance with our definition of culture as a form-of-life that, in the end, escapes control. Secondly, civilizations do not have a simple or pure origin. As Durkheim and Mauss state: 'the myths, tales, money, commerce, fine arts, techniques, tools, language, works, scientific knowledge, literary forms, and ideas – all these travel, and are borrowed'.[7] In terms of dealing with culture as a form-of-life, cultures are a matter of creative *bricolage*: they do not come out of the blue but may use existing material for different purposes. Thirdly, a culture as civilization will have symbolic boundaries, but these need not be fixed; a culture can be appropriated, and it can infiltrate other societies. This is in accordance with considering culture in terms of change. Fourthly, and most important in the context of this chapter, money and commerce are driving symbols and define much behaviour in the spreading of civilizations and their interactions. Indeed, important motives of why peoples and cultures interact, is that they are driven by interests. Here, the Durkheim and Mauss conveniently overlooked the fact that this dynamic is often framed by, or orchestrated by imperial powers, like colonial ones.

If to Durkheim and Mauss the dynamics inherent to civilizations and their interactions with one another were flexible and fluid, this found a

5   Durkheim and Mauss, 'Note on the Notion of Civilization'. Originally published as 'Note sur la notion de civilisation', *L'Année sociologique* 12 (1913): 46-50.
6   Swedberg, 'A Note on Civilizations and Economies'.
7   Durkheim and Mauss, 'Note on the Notion of Civilization', 153; quoted in Swedberg, 18.

counterpoint in an influential study by political theorist Samuel Huntington (1927-2008). It was called *The Clash of Civilizations and the Remaking of World Order* (1996; first explored in an article from 1993). Huntington responded to an equally influential study by Francis Fukuyama, another political theorist, whose article was called 'The End of History?' (1989). Applying a Hegelian analysis of history as a form of struggle between parties that would be solved eventually by general agreement, Fukuyama argued that the collapse of Soviet-dominated communism and the turn of communist China towards capitalism at the end of the 1980s had dissolved all ideological struggle. Western-style liberal democracy was the endpoint of history.

Many have mentioned by now that Fukuyama was proven wrong[8] and he himself admitted his own miscalculation.[9] Just as many missed his reflections on the weaknesses of Western democracies towards the end of his study. Perhaps, precisely these were a motivation for the response by Huntington who stated that:

> the fundamental source of conflict in this new world will not be primarily ideological or primarily economic. The great divisions among humankind and the dominating source of conflict will be cultural. Nation states will remain the most powerful actors in world affairs, but the principal conflicts of global politics will occur between nations and groups of different civilizations.[10]

Although this quote insinuates that the clash between civilizations is one between equals, Huntington's study reproduced hierarchies that were familiar in modern Western history. They can be traced in his assumption that some civilizations are superior to others, whilst those others are implicitly or explicitly defined as 'backward'. Both Fukuyama's and Huntington's theories involved a culturalization of politics, as analyzed by Wendy Brown (cf. Chapter 4), that placed Western civilizations in a central position and other cultures in a marginal one. By now, this central position has become untenable for scholarly, ethical, and political reasons. The global balances of power have changed considerably in the last two decades.

---

8   One of the earliest authors to notice this was Paul Hirst, in an article published in *Open Democracy* in 2019 (Hirst, 'Endism').

9   Many interviews given after Fukuyama published later books testify to his retraction; see, for instance, Portland Aristotle, 'The Rise of China'.

10   Huntington, 'The Clash of Civilizations?', 22.

The image that functioned as a epigraph to this chapter alluded to one of the most famous works of classical music of the twentieth century: *Le sacre du printemps* (*The Rite of Spring*) by the Russian/French/American composer Igor Stravinsky (1882-1971). Born in Russia, he would develop a career in France first, and later in the United States of America. The piece was performed for the first time in Paris in 1913, accompanied by a ballet by the Russian dancer and choreographer Vaslav Nijinsky. He used costumes that resembled peasants' dress and had designed a ballet inspired by so-called 'tribal' dances. The performance turned into a scandal, people started fights on sight and the orchestra was targeted with vegetables. One reason may have been that parts of the audience were provoking a riot, but another certainly was that the play did not fulfil the expectations of an audience that wanted to see its particular conception of civilization represented. The critic of the major French newspaper *Le Figaro* called the performance a 'laborious and puerile barbarity'. Here it is, once again: the analogy between barbarism and childhood.

The hierarchies implicit in the term 'civilization' depend on the values one is attached to and the ideologies one clings to. Both verbs, 'attached to' and 'cling to' point to something that was often overlooked in the field of critical theory. Classic forms of critique of ideology would point to the fact that people may have wrong or false ideas about reality, the implication being that if they only could be led to the light, the problem would be solved. Apart from the fact that what is considered to be right or wrong, false or proper, may differ depending on the position one takes, this approach misses a pivotal consideration: the fact that values and ideologies are dominated less by ideas than by what one is attached to, or clings to. These are matters of emotions and affects.

5.2.   How are the interests of people defined by affects and emotions?

Yeah, yeah, yeah, yeah, yeah
Yeah, yeah, yeah, yeah, yeah
Yeah, yeah, yeah, yeah, yeah
Yeah, yeah, yeah, yeah, yeah

Stack my money fast and go (Fast, fast, go)
Fast like a Lambo' (Skrrt, skrrt, skrrt)
I be jumpin' off the stage, hoe (Jumpin', jumpin', hey, hey)
Crowd better savor (Crowd goin' ape, hey)

> I can't believe we made it (This is what we made, made)
> This is what we're thankful for (This is what we thank, thank)
> I can't believe we made it (This a different angle)
> Have you ever seen the crowd goin' apeshit? Rah

'Apeshit' by the Carters (2018)[11]

People's interests are inevitably affectively charged, and charged culturally. In line with the questions that opened the previous part, two other telling questions are: when do you drink your tea, and what kind of tea is that? Do you add milk, or does adding milk feel like an abomination? Do you feel that making and drinking tea is a pivotal element of your life, or does tea not interest you a single bit? If you live in China, Japan, or the United Kingdom, tea might be vital to the organization of your day, though it would concern different kinds of tea, and different kinds of organization of the day. If you reside in Colombia, tea might not interest you all that much. The answers depend on the interest you take in tea, or how tea is of interest to the culture you are part of.

The multiple reasons of interest function as the pivot between culture and economy. Economically speaking, interest is equivalent to *rent* as in a yearly rate of interest, but one can also take an interest in a company, for example, when one buys shares. Thus, interest deals with economic involvement that is preferably profitable, but may also be costly. In a more general sense, one can take an active interest in something when one is curious to learn, or when one wishes to participate. As a verb, interest implies that one provokes someone's interest, as in: 'I think this might interest you.' In all cases, the concept that was central to the previous chapter plays a role: value.

This is how economists Michael Hutter and Bruno S. Frey define value:

> While economic value finds expression in units of currencies which are generated and maintained by banking systems, cultural value finds expression through mutual, collective judgment procedures. Such judgments of relative value are communicated by media like audience applause, expert reviews, prizes, or length of text and footage dedicated in print and broadcast media.[12]

Hutter and Frey underestimate the role of culture, here, due to their economic perspective, in stating that what people value is only determined by

---

11   The Carters, 'Apeshit'.
12   Hutter and Frey, 'On the Influence of Cultural Value', 35.

media and their forms of communication. The 'mutual, collective judgment procedures' become operative, however, once human beings are thrown in the web of culture and become part of its repeated enactment. As a result, they become 'interested', which emphasizes that value is of interest to them: what they gain from it, how it makes them feel, and how it determines their sociocultural being. Although there is a rational aspect to interest, it is predominantly a matter of affect.

There is little doubt whether culture and its values and interests define human behaviour. They also direct much of our subconscious decisions, though it is up for debate as to how that exactly happens. The French psychologist and marketing consultant Clotaire Rapaille was at the heart of such a debate. According to Rapaille, the most basic part of our brain, the reptile part, is a powerful affective force that is imprinted with cultural values from an early age, and this imprint takes the form of a 'culture code'.[13] When the Swiss-based company Nestlé, a food producer with a strong focus on coffee and chocolate, asked Rapaille how to generate more revenue in Japan, he responded that Japanese people have no coffee imprint. His analysis was controversial because he seemed to view culture as resembling a person, and, moreover, a person with a certain essence. However, on the basis of the definition we use, any Japanese preference for tea or aversion against coffee, would not be determined by some cultural essence and an imprinted code, but on the basis of the fact that values are time and again, repetitively performed.

Such performativity is never determined by one monolithic entity, be it a culture or an economic system. Inevitably, things are much more dynamic and complex, as was demonstrated by the economic geographers Julie Graham and Katherine Gibson, or J.K. Gibson-Graham (cf. previous chapter). They described a diverse economic field in which:

> non-market transactions and unpaid household work (both by defini-
> tion non-capitalist) constitute 30-50% of economic activity in both rich
> and poor countries. [...] Such quantitative representations exposed the
> discursive violence entailed in speaking of 'capitalist' economies, and
> lent credibility to projects of representing economy differently.[14]

When analyzing the force field of diverse economies, it is inevitable that the analysis is based on specific interests itself. Likewise, as explained earlier,

---

13   Rapaille, *The Culture Code*.
14   Gibson-Graham, 'Diverse Economies'.

the study of culture cannot be based on an objective analysis. Matters become all the more complex, then, once we look at the interaction between cultures and economies. In dealing with this complexity, it is of importance to note that people often tend to know and feel what they are doing, but their actions may be ambiguous at the same time. According to the cultural analyst Sigmund Freud (1856-1939), this ambiguity tends to be fundamental to, and operative in how people live their culture.

Freud published a study in 1931 entitled *Das Unbehagen in der Kultur* (The unease in culture) that was translated as *Civilization and Its Discontents*.[15] Note how 'culture' and 'civilization' are used interchangeably once again. However, the choice for civilization may be functional in this case, because it emphasizes that cultures civilize people: they force them to behave. This is captured by the *form* part of 'form-of-life'. More so, this force also provokes a counter-reaction. According to Freud, the structure of civilization/culture counteracts the instinctive desires of individual human beings and the repression of these desires and feelings will lead to an organized life that is simultaneously troubled by forms of discontentment. On the one hand, civilization/culture should protect people against unhappiness, or it should foster the pursuit of happiness. On the other hand, precisely because culture forces people to behave in a certain way, it is also a force that can make people unhappy.

The terms used so far – *Unbehagen*, unease, discontent or discomfort, desires, instincts, happiness, feeling – all indicate that cultures are organized affectively, as are economies. This provokes the question of how to define this term 'affect'. The latter concerns an entity's or being's power to sense and to affect others. Alternatively, it concerns the entity's capacity to sense what is being done to it – how it is affected. This definition of affect is based on the ideas of the already mentioned Spinoza and French philosopher Gilles Deleuze (1925-1995). The primary point of departure for both of them was not so much ideas, but the materiality of things and bodies. Bodies are not merely rational entities in space towing a certain worldview; rather, they find themselves in a world full of relations which affect them. Bodies and minds are always affected and affecting.

There is a pivotal contrast to emotions, here, which can be traced by distinguishing between content and expression; terms which are dependent on form, matter, and substance. Suppose you have a fixed job that you like, a mortgaged house, and a new partner with three kids. Now, whether or not a person is able to cover or share costs much depends on

15   Freud, *Das Unbehagen in der Kultur* and *Civilization and Its Discontents*.

income, so you are in trouble when you go to work one morning and upon entering your office, you are told that you have to clear your desk within two hours since you just got fired. This is a *formal* thing; it involves *matter* (things you have to remove) and *substance* (your job) and its contents will be immediately clear. The question is: what does it *express*? The impact is instantaneous and affects your body and mind prior to you being able to process it. This is the plane of affect. Depending on how it affected you, a rush of emotions may take place: you may feel pain, you may feel scared, confused or worried, numbed, or sad. This, then, is the plane of emotions. Of course, you ask why you got fired. They tell you that the company has to downsize because of spiralling costs. Now you know that your being fired expresses you belonged to the ones who cost too much. Suppose that, later on, you discover that the company also made an enormous profit that same year. Now your being fired expresses something else. This will probably affect you in turn, because you start to relate differently to the event. Emotionally speaking, the results may also vary, from indignation to anger, from depression to disgust.

Affect has been considered to be in much closer proximity to emotion in the Anglophone world than in continental Europe. The reason for this is that English has terms like 'affection', 'an affective relationship', and so forth. Given this line of thought, affect connotes expressible feelings, emotions, and libidinal economies. Paradigmatic figures here are Eve Kosovsky Sedgwick (1950-2009), who was important in the field of queer theory; and Sara Ahmed, who was, and still is, influential in the field of diversity and inclusivity. For the other line of thought, affect rather connotes the inexpressible, it implies bodily intensities, and societal and ecological relations of any kind. Paradigmatic figures are the already mentioned Deleuze, who is influential in the conceptualization of desire; and Lauren Berlant (1957-2021), who is important in the field of economic systems and how these organize people's affective households.

We use emotion and affect to distinguish between how people feel to be moved (emotions) or feel to be driven (affects). The distinction between the two can be traced through the way in which people deal with relations. When they say they have a relationship, this is distinctly erroneous. The relation itself is precisely what one cannot *have*. One finds oneself *in* a relationship. Affects are the determinants of relations that drive people. People can *have* emotions; as if these are their own. They may share them, but emotions may also differ immensely. The same holds for affects. People can be in a relation together while being affectively involved differently, and while being moved by radically different emotions.

This part of the chapter opened with the song 'Apeshit' (2018) by The Cart-ers (also known as Beyoncé and Jay-Z). Several sites do not show the title of the song explicitly. The letters 'h' and 'i' are replaced by two asterisks. Apparently, the word 'shit' is not acceptable to some because of the affects it evokes. The clip that accompanied the song was shot in the French symbol of civilization and culture: the Louvre Museum in Paris. In the context of this chapter, we can analyze the song and clip on the basis of the interests involved, and the affects and emotions they imply. Some will want to take into account that, according to *Forbes* magazine, the 2019 net worth of the couple was $1.4 billion.[16] Others will want to emphasize that the couple's music has become an icon for current consumer culture. Still others will be fascinated by the way in which the couple deals with the Louvre as an icon of civilization, or how they promote another kind of civilization by re-contextualizing many of the paintings and statues shown. In any case, it will be impossible to deal with this piece outside of the complex affective and emotionally coloured relations between culture and economies.

This is the end of our discussion of the interaction between culture and economies. In Chapter 6, which concludes the first part of this introduction, we move to religion in order to assess its interaction with culture in terms of communities.

---

16   For a critical assessment of clips such as these, see hooks, 'Beyoncé's *Lemonade*'.

6.   Culture and Religion: Community

6.1.   What is the relation between culture, religion, and communities?

Amazing grace

How sweet the sound

That saved a wretch like me

I once was lost

But now I'm found

Was blind, but now I see

'Twas grace that taught

My heart to fear

And grace my fears relieved

How precious did

That grace appear

The hour I first believed

'Amazing Grace' by Aretha Franklin (1972)[1]

The distinction between culture and religion is notoriously difficult to make. Still, the reason they do not equate or should not be conflated, is proven by three facts. First of all, one culture can encompass many different religions. In the Dutch case, for instance, culture encompasses Protestants (of different kinds), Catholics (of different kinds), Muslims (of different kinds), Jews (of different kinds), and a variety of other religions, plus those who oppose any belief in a supreme being (atheists) or neither acknowledge nor deny the existence of a supreme being (agnostics). Secondly, a proselytizing religion – a religion that wants to spread its message to others – can gain followers in different cultures. In the last decades, for instance, we have witnessed the substantial growth of so-called Pentecostals and Evangelicals in radically different cultures, such as the French, Brazilian, or South Korean. Thirdly, a religion can become diasporic, which means that the religion itself does not desire to acquire new followers in different cultures, but rather moves through them, or exists within their context. Judaism is a primary example here as a paradigm of what is called diaspora or dispersion.

---

1   Franklin, 'Amazing Grace'.

That culture and religion can be conflated was highlighted in 1555, when, after almost a century of religious conflicts, the Peace of Augsburg was signed in Germany. The new balance consisted in the acceptance of what was captured by a Latin phrase: *Cuius regio, eius religio*. That is: whose realm you find yourself in, marks your religion. Rulers could decide which religion was dominant in their territory and then there were two options: Roman Catholicism and Lutheranism. If people did not want to comply, they were allowed to leave, but they would have to leave their property behind. If currently the south of Germany is predominantly Roman Catholic with considerable Protestant pockets, this shows how the consequences can still be traced more than four and a half centuries later.

Yet if culture seems to be a persisting force throughout the centuries, it is also of interest to look at Germany's eastern part, the territory of the former communist German Democratic Republic. In less than 50 years, between 1945 and 1990, when Germany was reunited, people apparently lost their religion. Moreover, as historian Thomas Grossbölting argued in a study entitled *Losing Heaven: Religion in Germany since 1945*, Germany has been secularizing rapidly, as a result of which the fabric of society has also changed.[2] Still, the secularization of Germany as a whole does not mean that the cultural differences between different regions also have disappeared.

If culture and religion are not to be conflated, they can be distinguished if we consider them not to be separate domains, but as the basis on which communities and selves organize and manifest themselves depending on the situation. Members of a specific community in the Netherlands can define themselves as Protestants, for instance, but when Dutch people from different backgrounds find themselves in Mumbai, we speak of a Dutch community. The same holds for individual selves, which we will discuss in the second part of this course, in Chapters 7 to 12. The current Chapter 6 concludes – after nation-state, world, society, and civilization – with this fifth notion of collective being: community.

'Community' is derived from Latin *communitas*, which again is derived from *communis*: that which people have or hold in common. The German term *Gemeinschaft* and Dutch *gemeenschap* indicate the same. The German sociologist Ferdinand Tönnies marked the difference between community and society in a study from 1887, as the difference between a collective bound by intimate relations based on forms of familiarity (*Gemeinschaft*,

---

2   Großbölting, *Losing Heaven*.

community), and one based on relations of interest (*Gesellschaft*, society).[3] According to his analysis, the explosive developments of trade and industry, driven by the amalgamation of modernity and colonialism, led to the dominance of society over community.[4] Consequently, the very idea of community became nothing more than a fiction on this larger scale. Nevertheless, this was a powerful fiction, as we saw when dealing with the nation-state. In fact, many conceptualizations of the nation still follow a community logic. In contrast, religion, even world religions with billions of believers, may have a top-down structure but are basically organized through small-scale communities. This led sociologist Robert Putnam to state that the communal is at the core of religions.[5]

The individual members of religious communities have in common a mixture of belief and faith, of religious doctrine, codifications, practices and rituals. What we consider to be belief is a matter of convictions, of what people hold to be true or truthful. It concerns, for instance, the conviction that Jesus is God and was resurrected, or that the Qur'an contains the direct word of God as it manifested itself through Muhammad. Faith is a matter of trust that one is not alone in the world. People have faith, for instance, when they trust that God will come to their aid. Religion is derived from the Latin *religare*, which means 'to bind'. Originally it indicated that people lived according to a certain rule, which was the basis of a form-of-life. In the course of history, however, religion came to mean an institutionalized and hierarchized form of belief. It was this power that came to define codifications and rituals as expressions of belief. For instance, depending on the religion people adhere to, this determines whether they are allowed to pray *to* a crucifix or only *with* a cross, or without one.

The origin of religion very much resembles that of community, if we analyze it according to how philosopher Roberto Esposito considered community as a composite of *cum* (with) and *munus*, which means 'burden' or 'task'.[6] Consequently, a community is not something that people positively and commonly share, but something to which they feel themselves obligated. It is this obligation that is at the basis of any community's strength.

The concept of community became the centre to debates in the 1990s, which reflected on the collapse of communism, and considered whether

---

3   The first English translation of the book (in 1955) translated *Gesellschaft* as 'association' (Tonnies, *Community and Association*). Later versions have opted for 'civil society' (for example, Tonnies, *Community and Civil Society*).

4   For a reconsideration of Tönnies' ideas, see Adair-Toteff, 'Ferdinand Tönnies'.

5   Putnam, *Bowling Alone*.

6   Esposito, *Communitas*.

there would be a viable alternative to the atomism or radical individualism of modern Western societies. Some considered community to be the
collective alternative to the individual self. However, as Esposito argued,
a community is not a subject. In a sense repeating Freud's argument that
culture has an alienating force, Esposito argued that a community places a
demand from the outside on an individual. Fulfilling this demand implies
that the individual becomes 'part of' a community, which in turn has an
empowering effect on the collective of individuals.

Community empowerment has been at the heart of several decolonial
attempts to counter the devastating effects of the modernity-colonialist
dynamic. For instance, in departments of health in Canada,[7] or of psychology in South Africa, scholars started looking for ways to think about and
conceive of communities that would do justice to the ways in which people,
whether indigenous or not, have shaped their communities under duress.[8]
Due to the effects of modernization and colonialism, such communities
need not be defined by people's origins. The concept of *nepantlism* was
central, for instance, in the work of Chicana anthropologist Gloria Anzaldúa.
The concept is derived from the Nahuatl word *nepatl*, which means: in the
middle. The term was consciously aimed at defining individual people
as actors moving through different worlds, not ultimately marked by the
collective they belong to, which in the end would often lead to an either/
or divide.[9] This is why Anzaldúa's approach was also called a 'borderland
theory', with the central concept of *mestizaje*; a concept that emphasized
how people often embody and live perhaps conflicting, perhaps intersecting
identities in contemporary circumstances. This does not mean that such
people have no communities they want to respond to. However, these need
not be defined by religions and the either/or dynamic these install.

The concept of community is complexified even more when considering the element of spiritualism, which is not only something by means of
which people may form a community, but also something that can imply a
community that entails both the dead and the living. Spiritualism can be
considered, on the one hand, as a regular aspect of any kind of religion, or as

7   For an overview, see Narasimhan and Chandanabhumma, 'A Scoping Review of Decolonization'.
8   One example is South African psychologists Floretta Boonzaier and Taryn van Niekerk's
book, *Decolonial Feminist Community Psychology*.
9   The influential French sociologist Émile Durkheim (1858-1917) developed a theory that
religion and society were effectively one and the same. Communal identity and group solidarity
weren't just affected by religion or aspects of it – they were at its very heart and purpose. Religions
functioned to unite and bind together community, thus dividing an 'us' and 'them' in moral
terms. See Durkheim, *The Elementary Forms of Religious Life*.

a necessary component, since it concerns the belief that there is more to the world than everyday reality. On the other hand, spiritualism also has more fundamental implications when it is at the basis of an entire lifeworld and considers spirits to be able to intervene in the world of everyday reality. When the work of Colombian author Gabriel García Márquez became famous in the West, his work was often considered to be part of what literary scholars called 'magic realism' because of the role spirits played in it. In the Western context, spirits were considered a matter of fiction. But perhaps for Márquez spirits were not a matter of fiction, but of reality. As such, spiritualism has been approached with suspicion by many religions, since it tended to spiral out of control of doctrinal requirements and limits. Generally, spiritualism indicates the human capacity to experience other realities, which is also why modern science has tended to view it with suspicion. Most scholarly responses to Anzaldúa's work, for instance, ignored the decisive spiritual elements of her work.

We started this chapter with a song sung by Aretha Franklin (1942-2018): 'Amazing Grace'. The song itself is an example of the dynamic between culture and religion and the distinction between them. The text was written by the Englishman John Newton (1725–1807), who first opposed any kind of religion and busied himself with the slave trade. He ended up swapping sides: he rejected the slave trade and confessed himself to the Anglican Church. The text was then set to an already existing tune by American composer William Walker. This version is popular among many different cultures and subcultures, but it is surely a musical icon in African-American Protestant circles. Aretha's father was a minister in the Baptist Church, and not only was he a star in giving sermons, but also in giving sermons that would fluidly morph into singing sessions. Such singing is neither purely religious, nor only a matter of belief and faith. It is as much a spiritual issue. This spiritual force, and the cultural tradition in which it is anchored, was taken up again by American president Barack Obama when he joined the burial ceremony of Clem. C. Pinckney in June 2015 and at some point started to sing this very song. Pinckney was a member of the South Carolina Senate and pastor of a community in the city of Charleston. He was killed in his own church, as one of nine people, by a 21-year-old man who believed in white supremacy. It is yet another indication of how culture can be a matter of belief, of faith, or of doctrine.

In the next part we will consider in more detail how religions can infiltrate other domains of life and become driving forces in how people are taught and required to behave. Religions will not prove to be ultimately determining forces here. We can safely say, based on an abundance of historical instances, that human beings are what they are: animals driven by desires and fears, impulses and restrictions, decencies and perversions. Even if they confess themselves to a certain religion, and the customs this allows and prohibits, they may behave differently nevertheless.

6.2.   How can separate domains of life infiltrate one another?

> Empty spaces, what are we living for?
> Abandoned places, I guess we know the score, on and on
> Does anybody know what we are looking for?
> Another hero, another mindless crime
> Behind the curtain, in the pantomime
> Hold the line
> Does anybody want to take it anymore?
>
> The show must go on
> The show must go on, yeah
> Inside my heart is breaking
> My makeup may be flaking
> But my smile, still, stays on
>
> 'The Show Must Go On' by Queen (1991)[10]

As may have become clear in the previous chapters, we can distinguish between domains or realms of life, such as culture, politics, economics, or religion. However, this does not mean that all these domains exist as separate entities. Rather, they constantly influence one another.[11] A radical manifestation of such influence occurs when one domain starts to infiltrate others with an air of superiority. This can happen, for instance, when the political domain frames religion to be scrutinized or undesirable, as happened in communist Eastern Europe, in the Soviet Union, or communist China. Given this context, it was a decisively political move by the Roman Catholic Church to elect a Polish pope in 1978. Cardinal Karol Józef Wojtyła (1920-2005) became John Paul II when the Roman Catholic Church was still suffering from suppression in the communist world. Obviously, this also

---

10   Queen, 'The Show Must Go On'.
11   Walzer, *Spheres of Justice*.

works the other way around, as is evident from the Hindu state India, or the Buddhist state Myanmar. In the seventeenth-century Dutch Republic, Calvinists tried to turn it into a so-called theocracy, just as Oliver Cromwell did in England. It would have been a form of government dominated by religious principles, institutions, and rulers. Since the revolution under Ruhollah Khomeini in 1979, Iran is an example of a mixture of theocracy and democracy. Recently Afghanistan may have joined the ranks of such states.

The period of the Enlightenment in the eighteenth century witnessed the principal separation of church and state. This was partly because religious conflicts had ripped apart entire European societies, and partly driven by a desire to create an autonomous domain of political decision making. This meant that religions could be practiced publicly, but ultimately peoples' beliefs became a private matter, not a matter of the state. The reverse, of course, implied that religion, as a private matter, should not interfere with public affairs.

Another form of infiltration was traced by the sociologist Max Weber in a study entitled *The Protestant Ethic and the Spirit of Capitalism*, from 1904. Weber was studying the cultural roots of the economic system prevailing in Western Europe and America and was asking the relevant question: why did capitalism become successful in Europe? Additionally, why were Protestants more prominently capitalist in northern Europe than Catholics in the south? The answer that Weber came up with made cultural historian Peter Burke comment that Weber's essay 'might equally well have been entitled "Capitalism and the Culture of Protestantism" or "Protestantism and the Culture of Capitalism"'.[12] Whereas Burke's remark makes clear that different domains can influence one another, it is also an example of how concepts can become blurred, as in 'the culture of Protestantism' and 'the culture of capitalism'. It makes more sense to speak of German or Dutch or English, or north-western European cultures in their relation to a religion and an economic system. Weber was indeed so precise in assessing the role of a Protestant, more specifically a Calvinist, ethos or value system in relation to the accumulation of capital.

Weber claimed that sixteenth-century Calvinism, rather than Lutheranism, is decisive for the *Geist* of capitalism. Firstly, this is due to its asceticism and individualism; secondly, due to the, theologically speaking, fundamental uncertainty as to whether one belongs to the chosen people or not; an uncertainty that needs to be countered by secular success. Very much like Cromwell in England or the Dutch Calvinists, German Calvinists lived and

12   Burke, *What Is Cultural History?*, 10.

propagated a sober life, rejecting any form of exuberance. This economic attitude resulted in frugality and savings which people could use in the market. Calvinists rejected the authority of the Roman Catholic Church, any church in fact, because the individual believer already had access to the word of God through the Bible. This strengthened their individual undertakings. Theologically speaking, Calvinism was determined by the doctrine of predestination, which postulated that the sovereign God had complete providence. Each individual's fate, whether one belonged to the chosen or not, had already been decided upon prior to one's arrival. Hence, the only undetermined achievement left was the alternative of secular success.

Weber was concerned with capitalism, not with the role of religion in society. Consequently, he did not consider the concept of *Beruf, Berufung*, or 'calling' to be important, as it was coined by Martin Luther (1483-1546). The concept was based on Greek χλῆσις (*klēsis*), Latin *vocation*, and it had been a prominent concept from St. Paul in the first century to Luther in the sixteenth. Both held that any worthy action in a societal context would be an answer to a divine call. Making daily life a matter of religious concern through *Beruf* implied the equalization of spiritual and material affairs. This was not decisive for capitalism according to Weber, precisely because capitalists are not much concerned with general well-being.

For now, our question involves how religion can infiltrate cultural domains and on which bases. If we define cultures as a form-of-life, many of the forms are not prescribed beforehand. There is an aspect of arbitrariness to the form, to a extent. For instance, the customs by means of which people greet one another are variable and diverse. People can rub noses, they can raise a hand (whether this is the right or the left one), they can press their palms together in front of their breast, they can courteously bow, they may shake hands, or touch one another's elbows. Whichever one they decide upon, the ritual marks a culture. However, the choice for this form itself is not motivated beforehand, only in hindsight. People started doing something, which then attained a form. Only then did it require motivation. By implication, considered as form-of-life, cultures stand on their own feet. Religions, in contrast, always proclaim a double reality, of which one is of a higher and more powerful nature. Religions adhere to transcendence: that which goes beyond the limits of the given world. It is this otherworldly realm from which religions derive their authoritative voice, and which lets them claim the right to infiltrate other domains of life.

One theatre play is helpful in seeing how this occurs on a daily basis: Tony Kushner's *Angels in America: A Gay Fantasia on National Themes*.

The play consists of two parts: *Millennium Approaches* and *Perestroika*. It was published in book form in 1993 as a reflection on its own times, as the two titles suggest. In 1989, the Berlin Wall had fallen, as a result of which a political tension that had been dominant for half a century was defused. Communism lost its appeal, and communist states turned capitalist. In Soviet Russia, this was captured by a term coined by the Soviet leader of the time: Mikhail Gorbachev. 'Perestroika' stood for radical or structural reform. Then, in the last decade of the second millennium, there were more than enough people anxiously awaiting the year 2000. This anxiety was highly religiously inspired. Both Zoroastrianism and Christianity adhere to the belief that a divine organization of time relates to thousand-year periods. In Christianity this is called millennialism or chiliasm, indicating the belief that, prior to the final judgement, a golden age of a thousand years will come. Adolf Hitler also picked this format when he stated that Nazi Germany was the beginning of a *Tausendjähriges Reich* (a thousand-year empire).

The 'Gay Fantasia' of the subtitle was related to two different forms of American cultures at the time. On the one hand, there were the gay communities in the urban centres of America's East and West Coasts. On the other hand, the subtitle referred to what we may call the 'culture of a period': the 1980s and early 1990s. The latter reference was very much part of a US-dominated cultural atmosphere. It was the period of MTV, which became an incredibly important channel for youth culture after its launch in 1981. These were the times of Michael Jackson and Madonna, of hip-hop music and breakdancing, of Schwarzenegger and Stallone, of Indiana Jones and ET, with famous sitcoms such as *Cheers*, *The Cosby Show*, *Who's the Boss?*, and *Family Ties*. Last but not least, whilst the first prototype of the Apple personal computer had been developed in 1976, the Apple 'Classic' Macintosh, introduced in 1984, rapidly came to feed a mass market in the 1980s. In terms of atmosphere, these were the times of the beginning of neoliberalism, the fall of the Berlin Wall, of global protests against cruise missiles, the first space shuttle, Live Aid, of the Chernobyl disaster, the Tiananmen Square protest, of Deng Xiaoping (1904-1997) as the 'architect of modern China'. These years were also the cradle of an acronym that has become basic to many things: *www*, the World Wide Web, was introduced in 1989. Looking at these lists, not much religion is to be traced. Keep in mind though that we are looking at things here partly from a US American cultural industry perspective, and that a Polish pope was still the pope of the 1980s. With regard to the USA, there were two domains of life in which religion played a dominant role, related to two different forms of politics.

On the national level in the United States of America, Ronald Reagan was elected president in 1980, taking office in 1981. Only 69 days after he took office, an assault on his life was made on 30 March. He survived, telling the American audience that he had been saved by God. Two years later he delivered a speech (8 March 1983) to the National Association of Evangelicals, during which he referred to the Soviet Union as an 'evil empire'. By claiming the opponent to be evil, a political conflict was transformed into a moral and religious one. The phrase was repeated by George W. Bush (on 20 January 2002), when he defined three nation-states as an 'axis of evil': North Korea, Iran, and Iraq.

Then, gay communities in the urban centres of the United States were struck by a disaster in the beginning of the 1980s. The unknown virus, circulating under the acronym AIDS, haunts people globally up until today. At the time, the virus was new, had no cure, and caused a series of diseases that led to the entire collapse of the human body and ultimately death. It led to a paralyzing shock in the affected communities and their surroundings. It was also met by an all-too-expected religious response. Some considered the disease to be a punishment by God, or a deserved one, and this may explain why, on a political level, responses to the disease were slow. It was one more example of how religions may infiltrate other domains of life, in this case the domain of how people behave sexually. Whereas history offers ample evidence of a wide variety of sexual practices amongst human beings, some of which were even promoted by religions, there are also religions which prescribe a restricted set of such practices and consider all others to be morally wrong, hence to be prohibited.

We started this chapter with a song by Queen, 'The Show Must Go On', performed in 1990. A video recording of the show does not exist, because the singer, Freddie Mercury, born as Farrokh Bulsara (1946-1991), was too unhealthy at the time: he had already been suffering from AIDS for years. We hear Mercury sing: 'I'll soon be turning, round the corner now / Outside the dawn is breaking / But inside in the dark I'm aching to be free'. He died in November 1991. Considering that homosexuality had only been legalized in the United Kingdom in 1967, Mercury was well aware of what the price could be when one was publicly open about sexual practices. Being open about one's homosexuality could lead to fierce moral condemnation. However, to many it also entailed a personal liberation to do speak about things publicly, or act them out; a liberation that, in turn, could nurture a feeling of self that was much more one's own. We discuss different forms of selfhood and their relation to culture in Part 2: Cultural Selves.

Part 2

Cultural Selves

7. Culture and Self: Individuality

7.1. Why do people want to lose their selves, or sacrifice themselves?

> Comin' a time, B.D. women ain't gonna need no men
> Comin' a time, B.D. women ain't gonna do need no men
> Oh they way treat us is a lowdown and dirty sin
>
> B.D. women, you sure can't understand
> B.D. women, you sure can't understand
>
> They got a head like a sweet angel and they walk just like a natural man
>
> B.D. women, they all done learnt their plan
> B.D. women, they all done learnt their plan
> They can lay their jive just like a natural man
>
> B.D. women, B.D. women, you know they sure is rough
> B.D. women, B.D. women, you know they sure is rough
> They all drink up plenty whiskey and they sure will strut their stuff
>
> 'BD Woman's Blues' by Lucille Bogan[1]

The epigraph tune of this chapter was released by Lucille Bogan in a 1935 recording of 'BD Woman's Blues', with the BD referring to 'bulldyke women'. Bogan (1897-1948) was an African-American blues singer and songwriter, and one of the first to record blues songs, also under the pseudonym Bessie Jackson. Many of her songs were sexually explicit, which is why she is considered a significant contributor to the so-called 'dirty blues'.[2] Writer and critic Sasha Geffen wrote about the song:

> Music is a space where singers can say what they mean without saying it, where melody and rhythm offer plausible deniability for even the most plainly sung truths. 'BD women, you sure can't understand / They got a head like a sweet angel and they walk just like a natural man', openly

1 Centurion0192, *Lucille Bogan – B.D. Woman's Blues* (1935).
2 Wheeler, "Shave 'em Dry'", 161.

celebrated her butch and transmasculine siblings decades before the fight for LGBTQ rights had entered the mainstream.[3]

Geffen is also author of the study *Glitter up the Dark*, published in 2020. In this study Geffen asked: 'Why did the query "Is he musical?" become code, in the twentieth century, for "Is he gay?" Why is music so inherently queer?' Elsewhere, reflecting on the work of one of the great composers of electronic music in the 1960s, Wendy Carlos – born as Walter Carlos in 1939 – Geffen wrote:

> More than many other art forms, music is inextricably linked to the body. Singing issues directly from the diaphragm, lungs, throat, and mouth, and intermediaries like guitar and piano respond expressively to subtle variations in touch. Music, pop music especially, has historically served as an active staging ground for the reproduction and reinvention of gender. For cis musicians as well as trans ones, a stage or a recording studio can be a dream space where fantasy or deeply held personal truth can be acted out, surfacing in the timbre of a vocal take or the futuristic trill of a keyboard line.[4]

Tellingly, the title of her essay was 'Synthesizing Sound and Self', suggesting an intrinsic link between music and self, while at the same time embracing Carlos as an individual with a specific identity as transgender. This provokes the question: what is the distinction between individual, identity, and self – and how may these be culturally determined?

'Individual' literally means undivided, indicating that someone is one entity as an individual. The very term suggests an opposite in that there are entities which are divided: *dividuals*. This is indeed the case. The French philosopher Gilles Deleuze argued that congruent with the society of control that developed in the last decades of the previous century, people have increasingly become different sets of dividable data, which is what the term 'dividual' connotes.[5] This dynamic has only intensified with the advent of algorithms in social media, by means of which the people controlling them can feed their consumers with specific, tailor-made information. Such algorithms also form the basis for ethnic profiling; they do not consider any individual as such but rather as a set of statistically marked data.[6]

---

3   Geffen, 'How Pop Music'.
4   Geffen, 'Synthesizing Sound'.
5   Deleuze, 'Postscript on the Societies of Control'.
6   De Zeeuw, 'Encountering the Law'.

As we already noticed, culturally speaking, the notion of the individual is intrinsically connected to that of the collective. The value of the two considered separately and the balance or relation between them, is culturally specific (cf. Chapter 4) and almost always involves issues of identity. 'Identity' means that something or someone stays the same, which is also captured by the term 'identical'. One's name, for instance, stays the same throughout one's life and marks one's identity. That is to say: in contemporary times and in nation-states which register individuals and acknowledge them from birth. As this example illustrates, identity is not something individuals control themselves, for a name is first and foremost given and can only become a matter of choice later. Identity is very much related, that is, to what is given, by what is shaped and perceived by others. For instance, the American civil rights fighter Malcolm X (1925-1965) was named Malcolm Little at birth. Later in life he refused his family name, which was the name of a former slave owner, and chose to become Malachi Shabazz first, to then opt for crossing out his family name by the X. In the course of his life, when he turned towards Islam, and after he returned from a pilgrimage to Mecca, he re-named himself again as el-Hajj Malik El-Shabazz.

A less charged example may be that when people are asked what they 'do', they tend not to answer that they like sleeping for nine hours, love listening to music, or play squash – unless playing squash is their profession. In current circumstances, identity has come to be connected to one's profession, which is also why it may be a terrifying thing when people lose their job, since it feels like losing part of their identity. In terms of gender, identity became increasingly important over the last half century. With gender a distinction was made between what seemed to be essentially a biological given, but what were culturally determined forms of sexual behaviour, or roles.[7] The fact that these roles are culturally determined also led to recurrent and sometimes relentless debates about how to define such roles. For instance, when Bogan made her recordings in 1935, the term 'dyke' was used in some African-American communities, but was still slang to a general audience. The term was reappropriated as a positive marker of identity in the fight for LGBTQ+ rights that has been growing since the 1960s. When Facebook censured the term because they considered it 'abusive' in June 2017, this led to numerous protests.

7   An important study, originally published in 1990, was Butler, *Gender Trouble*. It was followed by an entirely new field of research, queer theory, and all sorts of debates in the LGBTQI+ movements.

There are still many cultures in which homosexuality has negative connotations, just as there are cultures or times in which the physical love between same-sex partners is a regular practice. There are also cultures in which the definition of masculinity or femininity is radically different from what recently used to be common Western usage. The film ALEXANDER by the American director Oliver Stone proves as much. This Hollywood production had great difficulty sticking to historical accuracy, in any sense of the term, but especially with regard to Alexander's sexuality; his sexual practices were rather flexible. Stone's or Hollywood's anxieties were determined by a long Christian history that silenced bisexuality or homosexuality, punished it, or reinterpreted it to hide its existence.

The latter happened when Christian commentators reinterpreted a Greek and Roman story about the most beautiful young man who lived on earth and who was taken up to heaven by Zeus to be – depending on the literary rendering – a cup-bearer at divine dinners, or Zeus' bedfellow. Christian commentators reinterpreted the story by considering the beautiful boy to be a template for the human soul that is carried to heaven by God. Nevertheless, the negative connotations of the story are still palpable if one knows that in the Roman version the name of the young man was Catamitus. This, in turn, led to the English pejorative term 'catamite', a negative marker of someone's job, or practice.

'Self' is less a matter of how someone is perceived or what someone expresses and more a matter of how people experience themselves internally. Transgender people often have the feeling, sometimes from a very young age, that they were born in the wrong body. Their sense of self does not coincide, then, with their body-mind experiences. In this case, there is a basic self that feels something does not fit. The opposite is that a feeling of self no longer exists, or is destabilized, as can happen in some psychological disorders that lead to a loss of self, for instance, when people do and experience things that do not feel as if they are connected to their selves.

The sense of self can be illustrated beautifully by the test of the mirror. Whereas it may seem self-evident that people recognize themselves in a mirror, this is actually something that only happens from a certain age onwards. The Russian director Viktor Kossakovsky made a documentary about his son Svyato, whose name is also the title of the work (2005).[8] Kossakovsky raised the boy in a house where all the mirrors were covered. Then, at age two, a life-sized mirror was uncovered, and the boy saw himself fully for the first time. He acted as if he was looking at another boy. Gradually, he learnt,

---

8   Kossakovsky, SVYATO.

as all people do, that the image on the surface was him: 'It's me' – a simple phrase that suggests a pivotal split: 'It' = 'me'. This does not imply that the boy only experiences a self when in front of a mirror. For the major part of history, people have lived without mirrors while experiencing forms of self. This is because their selves are determined by another kind of 'mirror', namely, the symbolic systems of power operative in any culture.

A basic example here is anyone's name. People feel that they name coincides with them. Yet it (again an 'it') was given to them and it took the first years of life to make the two coincide. It serves to show that people do not have an essential self from the start, but that they perform a self in given circumstances. This performance also concerns people's names, as all those can testify who did not like their name and changed it. Most of the time this is met with great resistance.

It is not just sexual practices that have changed considerably over time, and in different cultures. Time periods have their own cultural characteristics, and this includes specific forms of self. It led the Canadian philosopher Charles Taylor, in *Sources of the Self* (1989),[9] to locate the origins of the modern self in European Romanticism. Several conceptual ideas that Westerners now consider self-evident were invented at some point, as Taylor makes clear. One idea that they often take for granted is that people have an inward source; another one is that their self consists in the making of moral choices; a third is that they can express themselves; a fourth that the self is determined by forms of agency, of what the self can *do*; a fifth that life is valued for what it is in daily reality. If, indeed, most or all of these senses of self appear to be self-evident, it suffices to study other cultures in space or time. For eighth-century Vikings, moral choices would matter differently or the parameters of moral choices were markedly different; the ability to express themselves was different as well, or what one could or could not do, and all this related differently to how one felt one's self and how one was perceived.

Whereas according to Taylor, a 'deep' kind of self has become the centre of things since Romanticism, this stands in sharp contrast with almost all religions throughout history that have regarded the self to be a hindrance, precisely because it is too attached to reality, or everyday life. It is rather through a loss of self that people may get in touch with higher realities and spiritually different domains of life. In Buddhism, in Zen, or in Sufi traditions the self might dissolve, for example, through meditation, inactivity, or dancing. In Jewish mysticism, Christian mysticism, or shamanism, the self

9   Taylor, *Sources of the Self*.

could vanish by means of secret knowledge, mystic experiences or singing, or through the performance of certain rituals in combination with the use of drugs.

Culturally speaking, a loss of self can become alarmingly concrete when people are willing to sacrifice themselves, to give up their lives for the common, cultural good, for political reasons, or religious ones. For instance, the world witnessed the most disastrous nuclear disaster ever, up until today, in Chernobyl in 1986 (which at the time was part of the Soviet Union, but currently is part of Ukraine). The effects of this disaster still are still palpable four decades later, with large parts of the region remaining no-entry zones. At the time, however, the fear was that an even bigger explosion would occur, one that would contaminate half of Europe for decades to come. This did not happen, though, because people were willing to take actions to prevent that outcome, sacrificing their health and even their lives in the process. They may have done this for the greater good of humanity. Yet, the immediate impulse may also have been that they did this for their country, their people, their culture. Others did something similar in hope of a better future and out of protest, like Thích Quảng Đức, a Buddhist monk who burned himself alive in 1963 protesting the persecution of monks by the South Vietnamese government. More recently a Tunisian street vendor named Tarek el-Tayeb Mohamed Bouazizi burned himself to death on 4 January 2011, at the age of 26, because he could no longer cope with being humiliated by the police. His death sparked the Tunisian revolution that in turn set in motion the entire Arab Spring.

The epigraph of this part of the chapter is derived from a blues song by Lucille Bogan. A song may have a text that can express forms of self. Yet, as we saw with regard to Wendy Carlos, music per se also has an expressive ability to express a self. Carlos produced an album called *Sonic Seasonings* (1972; remastered and published under Carlos's new name in 1992), one of the first to introduce the New Age period with its interest in spiritualism. She also collaborated with director Stanley Kubrick for the soundtracks of the famous movies A CLOCKWORK ORANGE (1971) and THE SHINING (1980). Additionally, she developed the music of the Disney movie TRON (1982), which was considered as a prefiguration of early rave and hip-hop cultures according to critics. This type of music was aimed at a loss of self by way of musically induced ecstasy. TRON, moreover, introduced the science fiction motive of different forms of selves, involving artificial ones (cf. Chapter 12). A CLOCKWORK ORANGE and THE SHINING were a different matter, though. Whereas the loss of self is something that people want to engage in voluntarily, the next part of the chapter will address involuntary losses of self.

7.2. How can people become alienated from their culture?

> All I can ever be to you is a darkness that we knew
> And this regret I got accustomed to
> Once it was so right
> When we were at our height
> Waiting for you in the hotel at night

'Tears Dry on Their Own' by Amy Winehouse (2007)[10]

The lyrics of the epigraph song describe a particular scenario of a couple destined for trouble. Still, it may also capture a more common feeling of people living under modern conditions in major cities, in a 'darkness' that they know all too well. Somehow, they have the sense that things were 'right' in the past, but they no longer are. Ever since the middle of the nineteenth century, the conditions under which people live in modern urban environments have been described time and again in terms of their being out of sync, or in terms of straightforward alienation.

The first to analyze this trend was Karl Marx (1818-1883), who became famous for his critique of capitalism. However, he was not just being philosophically critical. He noticed the abysmal conditions under which millions of people had to live in the industrialized filthy, disease- and poverty-stricken overcrowded slums that surrounded urban centres, with people being exploited in ways that made any future seem hopeless. Workers were alienated from what their lives had been, in Marx's analysis. He did not pay much attention to culture, though it could have given his idea of alienation an even stronger underpinning. Instead, Marx defined alienation mainly socially, describing how people who used to have a sense of self and a sense of agency and control over their destiny were reduced to mechanistic labour forces in oppressive industries.[11] They were alienated from what they produced, from how they were making it, alienated from their sense of humanity and from relations with others. Culturally speaking, they came

---

10   Winehouse, 'Tears Dry on Their Own'.
11   Marx developed his ideas first in studies from 1844 that were published as *Economic and Philosophical Manuscripts: Early Writings*.

from rural areas most of the time. Although they would have had a poor existence there, they still had a living culture, which had now been replaced by an alienating urban situation ruled by economic or financial parameters.

Since the nineteenth century, modern life increasingly came to be determined by its massive scale. This can relate positively and negatively to a loss of self. It can relate positively to a loss of self in that urban life offers individuals the possibility of having a life of their own without anyone taking too much notice of it, which is a form of freedom.[12] Massive urban environments may relate negatively to people because the feeling of belonging to a living culture has evaporated in an atomized and massified society. The characteristics of these new masses were studied by sociologist Elias Canetti in a study from 1960 entitled *Masse und Macht*, or *Crowds and Power*.[13] Canetti noticed that:

- masses desire to grow;
- within masses equality rules;
- masses like density;
- masses move, and therefore need a direction.

In this context, one should not think of masses having some sort of self or identity, as cultural collectives have. First and foremost, masses are forms of undirected energy that work accordingly by means of equality and concentration, or indeed density, while desiring to expand and find a direction.

This is also why masses have been described in terms of inflation. The latter term currently has distinct economic or financial connotations, referring to a reduction in purchasing power, but originally it simply means that something grows because air is blown into it: *inflare* (an origin that connects inflation to flatulence). Masses have a desire to inflate, then, and they live in symbiosis with modern urban regions that keep inflating, sometimes on an hourly basis. In the last decade, for instance, the Nigerian city of Lagos grows with approximately 90 people entering the city per hour, not to visit but to live there. Lagos grows, or inflates, by around 2200 people per day.

If we think about masses in relation to culture, this often invites uniformity, whether in terms of urban architecture or in terms of the organization of the masses. Whether it concerned the great ideologies of capitalism,

---

12   Also see next chapter; Tonkiss, 'The Ethics of Indifference'.
13   Canetti, *Crowds and Power*.

communism, fascism, or Nazism: they all aimed to orchestrate and direct the power and lives of the masses by making them somehow uniform. This has not just led to the uniformity of living environments, what architect Keller Easterling called 'infrastructure space', but also a uniformity in the lives of individuals.[14] Or it led, perhaps paradoxically, to the industrialized or customized way in which any individual is made to feel like an individual person.

Next to the massive uniformity of humans, the make-ability of the self has provoked anxieties about the status of the modern self, when people wondered whether the human self is still really human. Culturally speaking, the number of representations pondering this issue has grown exponentially since the beginning of the nineteenth century. Mary Shelley's novel *Frankenstein* (1818) is a formidable point of departure.[15] A more recent reflection is BLADE RUNNER from 1981, which had a tag line that might as well have been that of *Frankenstein*: 'Man has made his match… Now it's his problem.'

The imagination of artificially made beings had the rhetorically reassuring effect of representing their makers, human beings, as somehow natural. Yet philosophers such as Slavoj Žižek or Roberto Esposito would dismantle such fantasies instantaneously. Žižek, in this context, contends the following:

> Therein consists the implicit philosophical lesson of BLADE RUNNER attested to by numerous allusions to the Cartesian *cogito* (like when the replicant-character played by Darryl Hannah ironically points out 'I think, therefore I am'): where is the *cogito*, the point of my self-consciousness, when everything that I actually am is an artifact – not only my body, my eyes, but even my most intimate memories and fantasies? [...] It is here that we again encounter the Lacanian distinction between the subject of enunciation and the subject of the enunciated: everything that I positively am, every enunciated content I can point at and say, 'that's *me*', is not 'I'; I am only the void that remains, the empty distance toward every content.[16]

Žižek begins with the famous observation by the seventeenth-century philosopher René Descartes, who defined that he knew he had a self because he was capable of thinking about what he thought. Subsequently, Žižek addresses the distinction between the subject of enunciation and the subject of the enunciated. With the first he indicated an 'I' that enunciates something.

14 Easterling, *Extrastatecraft*.
15 Shelley, *Frankenstein*.
16 Žižek, *Tarrying with the Negative*, 40.

It says, for instance: 'I think.' It is through saying this, however, that the subject constitutes the enunciated 'I'. In between this subject enunciating something and being enunciated, there is the void or the abyss of the self.

On a more general level, thinkers have traced a similar dynamic in the use of modern media. Though it seemed as if people were using such media, the equation could also be reversed: new media came to produce new forms of selfhood, sometimes with alternating positive and negative consequences. For instance, media scholar Marshall McLuhan (1911-1980) reflected on the effects of the medium of print. Print implied a shift from a society in which people would have a language collectively but live separate lives, to one that was highly influenced by a printing industry in its capacity to reach the masses:

> [T]he separation of the individual from the group in space (privacy), and in thought ('point of view'), and in work (specialism), has had the cultural and technological support of literacy, and its attendant galaxy of fragmented industrial and political institutions. But the power of the printed word to create the homogenized social man grew steadily until our time, creating the paradox of the 'mass mind' and the mass militarism of citizen armies. Pushed to the mechanized extreme, letters have often seemed to produce effects opposite to civilization.[17]

McLuhan points towards an intensely studied issue here: highly educated and cultured individuals have proven that they are capable of incredible atrocities once they become part of a uniformed mass that disengages or unhinges their moral selves.

With the advent of social media, this dynamic has acquired an even more ambiguous status. On the one hand, these social media platforms appear to be capable of addressing people individually, or of facilitating a sharper individual profile. Simultaneously, they allow people to play with their identity, as when individuals appear under a different user name. Yet such individuals could also be completely artificial, propelled by so-called 'bots'. And yet another matter is whether the individualized profiles are, in the end, not the result of a homogenous logic.

It is surely telling that a (small) number of people opt for a social media detox at times. The latter term suggests that different social media, somehow, have a poisoning effect. However, human beings have also proven to be a species that is able to deal with, or live with, addictions; perhaps it is even

---

17   McLuhan, *Understanding Media*, 116. Originally published in 1964.

incapable of living without addictions. One issue is, for instance, whether culture itself could not be considered a form of addiction – an issue yet to be explored in a scholarly way.[18] And then again, perhaps the question is always, rather, who benefits from certain addictions. In the case of social media, this question can be answered easily. For instance, the person who attacked the Christmas Market in Berlin, on 19 December 2016 – resulting in twelve deaths – took a selfie in front of German chancellor Angela Merkel's house two months earlier. Anis Amri may have been building his individual profile in the context of a much broader sociocultural and sociopolitical context; say, an online community. Perhaps he felt he would acquire a stronger self, through this selfie, with a marked religious and masculine identity. He was also one of millions of 'dividuals' feeding information to Facebook, renamed as Meta in 2021, which makes considerable profits with this information by selling it. The change of name of the corporation into Meta ironically makes it clear that the organization does not care much about human selves, but hovers above these selves.

We started this part of the chapter with a song by Amy Winehouse, about whom cultural theorist Daphne A. Brooks noticed with regard to Winehouse's 'spectacularly unorthodox and discontinuous engagement with retro forms and cultural nostalgia':

> The irony of Winehouse's work is that it generates its own form of aliena-tion effects. There is a way in which the dissonance of her persona and repertoire call attention to the process of 'cultural recall and forgetting'.[19]

Indeed, Winehouse worked with a public performance that seemed out of date and retro; with a 1950s beehive hair style and heavy eyeliner. Her public performances engaged with historically determined forms of identity. Yet her self was worked on by enormous social media pressures, as a result of which she could never be her own full self. Perhaps this is not new. Alexander the Great died at a fairly young age as well, after years of excessive drinking. He may have felt that he had to perform, had to be seen, had to be successful, publicly. He may have collapsed under these heavy burdens, or thought that drinking would help him deal with it. In terms of age, he outlived the infamous 27 Club. But then again, the '32/33 Club' might be bigger still.

18   Crocq, 'Historical and Cultural Aspects'.
19   Brooks, '"This Voice Which Is Not One"'.

With this, we wrap up the relation between self and identity. We move on to the relation between self and affiliation in the next chapter. The issue discussed will be to whom we think and feel we belong to or connect to, and to whom we do not. Affiliation is also a musical issue, by the way. For instance, in 1970 the American singer-songwriter Leon Russell (1942-2016) composed a song entitled 'A Song for You'. The song was covered by many artists, including Donny Hathaway (1945-1979), a member of the '33 Club'. His 1971 version, in turn, inspired Winehouse to make her own adaptation which was released in the 2011 album called *Lioness: Hidden Treasures*. The following lines in the song may be telling: 'I've acted out my life in stages / With ten thousand people watching / But we're alone now / And I'm singing this song to you'. With the arrival of social media, the question has become whether one can say that people are ever 'alone'.

8.   Culture and 'Other': Affiliation

Barricade during the Spartacus uprising, 12 January 1919[1]
Aram Kachaturian, 'Adagio' from *Spartacus* (1956)[2]

8.1.   Why do cultures construct an 'other' and what are the consequences?

This chapter deals with the issue of what people affiliate themselves to or with, culturally, and in that context focuses on dynamics of othering that have plagued cultural interactions for at least four centuries, as an intrinsic rhetorical and ideological tool of colonialism. More generally, we are dealing with the issues of whether human beings who feel themselves to be affiliated to a certain culture can escape the tendency to declare different cultures as 'other' or 'strange'; whether they can think of cultures interacting beyond hegemony and othering; or whether forms of hierarchy and othering are unavoidable. In order to deal with these questions, we need a concrete definition of what we mean by 'othering' and how the other differs from the figure of the stranger.

1   Verlag J.J. Weber. *Barrikade während des Spartakusaufstandes.*
2   Ballet by Khachaturian, *Spartacus.*

Hokusai, *Curious Japanese Watching Dutchmen on Dejima* (1802)[3]

The stranger can be seen as an equally important figure of modernity as the other. The stranger is neither an outlaw nor a wanderer, but 'the one who comes today and stays tomorrow', as sociologist Georg Simmel (1858-1918) defined it in a text entitled 'The Stranger'.[4] The basic element to Simmel was that the stranger is someone who comes, or arrives in an already existing situation. The Dutch were considered as such, for instance, when they arrived in Japan in the seventeenth century. They were not allowed to enter the Japanese territory any further than their base in Dejima, in Nagasaki – with Dejima meaning 'exit island'. The Portuguese had been there before, but had been expelled because of their attempts to spread

3   Hokusai, *Curious Japanese Watching Dutchmen on Dejima*.
4   Originally published in 1908 (Simmel, 'The Stranger').

Christianity. The Dutch had a sharper eye for their commercial interests, and had to bow to Japanese customs if they wanted to stay. So they bowed. Yet they remained strangers.

In the context of colonial agendas, the indigenous peoples of the Americas perceived the arrival of the Spanish distinctly as the arrival of strangers. And something similar happened in Japan when the Dutch arrived, as is captured in the woodblock print from 1802 shown below.

At the bottom left, someone is pointing at the strange people behind the wall. Precisely because the Dutch would remain strangers in Japan and would never rule it as a colony, they would never frame the Japanese as 'others', which is what they did do in the East and West Indies of their colonial empire.

Now the notions of 'stranger' and 'other' are often confused. This faux pas happened to Vince Marotta regarding one of the scholars studying the figure of the stranger, Zygmunt Bauman:

> Strangers threaten the boundaries that the ordering process requires in order to impose stability and predictability on the social world. In Bauman's words, strangers 'befog and eclipse the boundary lines which ought to be clearly seen'. [...] Strangerhood is articulated in multiple ways in Bauman's thought and different conceptions of identity underlie these multiple constructions. Bauman conceptualizes the stranger in terms of the social Other, links strangerhood to the Jewish experience in premodernity and modernity, implicitly connects the experience of strangeness to the hermeneutical problem, and links the stranger to existential experience.[5]

This quote does make it clear that strangers confuse the borders and the meaning of what seemed to be a common and stable world that became unsteady when some strange figure arrived. Yet the quote also confuses the stranger with the other, even with a capital 'O', which not only poses the question of how to distinguish between the stranger and the other but also between the other with a small 'o' and a capital 'O'. We will reconsider the figure of the stranger again in light of urbanism (cf. the second part of this chapter), and focus first on the other, with a small 'o' or a capital 'O'.

We reserve the other with a capital 'O' for a concept that was defined by the French philosopher Emmanuel Lévinas (1906-1995) in his study *Humanisme de l'autre homme* (1972, later translated as *Humanism of the*

---

5   Marotta, 'Zygmunt Bauman, 42. The quotes from Zygmunt Bauman are from his 'Making and Unmaking of Strangers', 1.

Other). In it, Lévinas developed an ethics that attempted to counter the idea that human beings had nothing but themselves on which to base their ethics. In line with this, he coined the notion of a radical Other, both a real and abstract entity. The notion connoted a meeting between self and other that would categorically question human beings from an external position and that could never be appropriated or instrumentalized for individual human needs. Thus, this Other was a 'radical other' that embodied an ethical demand beyond the human self.

The definition by Lévinas is decisively different from the one presented by Spivak. She published an article entitled 'Can the Subaltern Speak?' (1985) and elaborated her ideas in later works. Spivak dealt with the other as an ideologically produced other which fostered the construction of a superior European or Western self. This production excluded others from Western discussions, and prevented non-Europeans from holding positions as fully human subjects with equal rights. Her definition of the other distinguished between three dimensions that could also be used in circumstances that went beyond the colonial ones. The Danish sociologist Sune Qvotrup Jensen, for instance, used the concept to study how ethnic minorities in Denmark related to one another and to the dominant culture. He rendered the dimensions of Spivak as follows:

> The first dimension is illustrated by the English Captain, who travels around Sirmur on horseback to tell the natives, who their masters are. He describes in a letter how he journeys around colonial India to make the people aware 'who they are subject to'.

> The second dimension is illustrated in a letter from a General who writes about 'these highlanders' that 'I see them only possessing all the brutality and purfidy [sic] of the rudest times without the courage and all the depravity and treachery of the modern days without the knowledge of refinement'.

> The third dimension is illustrated in a letter from the Board of Control in the British East India Company which argues that the Indian Army in Colonial India should not be given access to knowledge and technology, i.e. 'the master is the subject of science or knowledge'.[6]

---

6   Jensen, 'Othering', 64-65. The quotes are from Spivak, 'The Rani of Sirmur', pp. 254, 254-255, and 256, respectively.

In this case, then, the other is not a radical Other, but a subject that is straightforwardly appropriated and degraded by a dominant force. It is a functional other, as a source of information, of labour or exploitation, as someone subordinate and morally inferior who by implication calls upon a supposedly morally superior ruler. The motivation for this dynamic in the colonial context may be clear. Quite a few countries in Europe granted themselves the right to appropriate enormous amounts of land and the territories of others. Ideologically they had to define such others as inferior, otherwise there was no legitimate underpinning of the appropriation.

Indeed, according to any standard of law or justice, the colonial thefts were indefensible; unless, of course, one defined others as inferior and uncivilized people, who needed to be included in the process of civilization, or whose lands could be taken because they clearly *belonged* to many, but were not owned. In this process, an even lower category than that of the other came into being: the subaltern. Spivak acquired this concept from the Italian philosopher Antonio Gramsci (1891-1937) and elaborated that this subaltern was a rightless, depoliticized subject, only good enough to do the dirtiest work. Here as well, the issue of interest is to consider whether contemporary societies have subalterns too, or still. Apart from the subaltern, another issue is how dominant cultures can use othering in the contemporary situation to remain dominant – a topic studied by Spivak in colonial and postcolonial times, and by Jensen in a so-called multicultural society.

The distinction between self and other as Spivak defined it, had implications for forms of knowledge production. This issue was also studied by the Palestinian-American literary theorist Edward Said (1932-2003) in a study entitled *Orientalism* (1978). Said researched the constructed ways of seeing the world, and focused on the perspective of colonizer more than on the perspective of the colonized. He showed how knowledge about the Orient was produced and constructed by the West and subsequently used to justify power relations. This led him to uncover the farce in Western humanism that suggested universal equality for all, but also veiled an ideology of superiority. Inspired by his study, different scholars set off to formulate the ideological counterpart of Orientalism. Ian Buruma and Avishai Margalit showed, in *Occidentalism: The West in the Eyes of Its Enemies* (2004), how Eastern cultures had their own ways of producing negative images of the West. For instance, the Japanese did not constrict the Dutch trading post for no reason; they viewed the Dutch as less civilized and culturally inferior.

The European colonial agenda led to the installation of new disciplines in the West, notably that of ethnography and anthropology, and the study of languages, like in Leiden, where Japanese, Chinese, and dozens of Indonesian languages were taught. The academic origin of these disciplines does not coincidentally correspond with the imperial wave of the second half of the nineteenth century. On the one hand, these new disciplines furthered the scholarly investigation of human sciences, and, on the other hand, they justified imperial expansion. Michel Foucault (1926-1984) was not alone in noticing that knowledge and power are strongly linked.[7]

In this context, Spivak's study *Death of a Discipline* (2003) provoked the question of how Western scholars from powerful academic institutes can willingly and consciously allow the other to enter the debate and how they can come to consider the other not just as a source of information but as a person to talk and listen to. Here she argued against an all too convenient kind of cosmopolitanism, as a matter of urban universalism:

> Politically correct metropolitan multiculturalists want the world's others to be identitarians; nationalist (Jameson) or class (Ahmad). To undo this binary demand is to suggest that peripheral literature may stage more surprising and unexpected manoeuvres toward collectivity.[8]

Spivak is dealing with the situation in the multicultural urban environments in global cities, here, and she is arguing against two scholars – Frederic Jameson and Sara Ahmed – who proposed that in such contexts the other is marked by an identity based on nationality or based on class. Instead, Spivak proposes not to set up such binary positions and to look for alternative perspectives in what she calls 'peripheral literature'. These are not literatures from the margin because the very term *peripheral* indicates that things have their own sphere.

The question Spivak implicitly poses is with whom scholars, or people in general, affiliate or disaffiliate themselves. Affiliation goes against any form of nationalism or straightforward biological relations. In Roman times, affiliation indicated that one could adopt someone as a son. This origin of the term points to the fact that family relations can be a matter of choice, though a matter of choice framed by the one who is doing the adopting. In turn, disaffiliation implies that one questions by whom or what one has been adopted, and makes a choice no longer to belong to this 'family'. The issue of affiliation and disaffiliation was pivotal in colonial contexts, in which people were forced to adopt another culture. In processes

---

7   Foucault, *Power/Knowledge*.
8   Spivak, *Death of a Discipline*, 55-56.

of decolonization people could then opt for consciously countering such adoption.[9]

Globally, right now, power dynamics are at work that are no longer dominated by former colonial powers, or by the West. Whether one takes the example of India, the different Islamic states in the Gulf region, or China, they all have their own excellent centres of knowledge and these centres have their own agendas. It is highly unlikely that in these centres of knowledge/power no forms of hierarchization will be involved. It is the case, for instance, that Chinese ideas of how the world should be ruled differ substantially from Western ideas. It is quite possible that the Chinese consider their ideas to be superior to the diverse Western ones.

The introduction to this part of the chapter showed a photograph of the so-called Spartacus uprising that took place in Germany in 1919, just after the First World War. The Russian-Armenian composer Aram Khachaturian (1903-1978) produced a ballet called *Spartacus* in 1954. This piece first of all thematized the great slave revolt that almost brought the Roman Empire to its knees; then, it implicitly glorified the Russian communist coup d'état in 1917; finally, it also alluded to this German uprising from 1919. In general, the piece supported the revolt of those suppressed by abusive powers. It would also become famous as the opening music for a highly successful English television series in the 1970s called THE ONEDIN LINE. The series sketched the history of a fictional shipping company based in Liverpool during the latter part of the nineteenth century. This was the heyday of British colonialism; yet the series only touches upon the colonial situation tangentially. This is one instance of the problem addressed by Spivak, that within a dominant Western position other voices have a hard time to be heard. Or, it proves the ethical necessity to involve all perspectives in the field of cultural interactions.

Whoever has watched Chinese blockbuster movies of the last two decades – for example, the sci-fi movie THE WANDERING EARTH (2019) – will have a similar concern, in that one culture is glorified and other perspectives are ignored. Apparently, many cultural actors operating in a global dynamic which is defined by many inequalities have this tendency to other others. This does not mean that scholars should adopt or support it in any way.

We will concentrate on yet another aspect of contemporary turbulences in the following part: modern urban environments and cultural hyper-diversity.

9   On disaffiliation, see Glissant, *Poetics of Relation*.

How are human selves defined in such situations of intensified cultural interactions and how are they able to affiliate themselves?

8.2.   How are selves defined in intensified urban situations of cultural interactions?

> Oh god. Geef mij kracht.
> Oh, geef mij kracht.
> Zo mooi als het woud is, zo gevaarlijk de vluchtroute
> Maar alles beter dan naar de baas terug te moeten
> Lang geleden dat ik vrij, vrijuit kon spreken
> Wij gaan niet terug, nooit meer terug
> We zijn er
> Hakbijl in de roos, of achilleshiel rad van fortuin spinnend wiel
> Tot de schroeven los gaan zitten
> Draai, Draai, als navigatiegestoorden, ik denk dat ik nog even blijf
> Wisselstoring, wisselstoring, en is het dat niet
> Is het wel zoiets als regen of wind
>
> 'We zijn er' by Typhoon (2014)[10]

Many peoples' lives are determined by the meeting of cultures while these are ordered hierarchically, within empires, between nation-states or ethnic states, or in contemporary multicultural urban environments. The colonial need for othering has not disappeared entirely in present-day circumstances. Instead, it has been replaced by procedures such as ethnic profiling. This happened to one of the most famous Surinam Dutch spoken-word artists in the Netherlands, Typhoon (Glenn de Randamie), in May 2016 (the epigraph of this section is taken from one of his songs). Typhoon reported the following via his Instagram account:

> I have just been stopped by the police in Zwolle. Not because of a traffic offence, but because my new car does not match my profile; in other words, how suspicious, a man of my color driving such a car. The officer on duty (friendly guy, by the way) admitted that he was prejudiced and considered that it could be drug money [that paid for the car]. Unfortunately, this is the umpteenth time this has happened to me, and I am 'famous', which

---

10   Typhoon, 'We zijn er'.

often makes the atmosphere much less tense after I've been recognized. Many don't have that privilege. Before, I was able to get angry about it, but now I already assume I will be stopped and actually become calm when it turns out, once again, that ethnic profiling is the reason. It is sad. I am choosing to share this now because this is not a singular event. It's not just the police; this is a big error in Dutch society. The first step towards change is admitting that racism/discrimination/differentiation is still a part of our culture. We're not even close yet! #ethnicprofiling #awereness #netherlands #racism #equality.[11] (Translated by Tessa de Zeeuw)

In the first building block of this study, we discussed *society* in relation to culture and considered how 'society' was the means for different cultures' living together without one dominant culture demanding subordination from others. The situation described by Typhoon rather relates to the nation-state; in this state there is this dominant culture, namely that of the nation. Here, there may be problems of so-called integration, which implies that other cultures have to adapt to, or assimilate in order to integrate. As ethnic profiling shows, however, the question is whether people can ever assimilate enough.

Still, we are also witnessing an ongoing process of rapid and massive urbanization, globally. In such circumstances, cultures may relate to one another in terms of a more negative or more positive indifference. The negative one can be described as a matter of alienation or estrangement. For instance, sociologist and educational theorist Shaun Best argues that 'fear of strangers involves a fear of strangeness and [...] the mechanisms that bring about a sense of community are the same mechanisms that generate estrangement'.[12] On the positive side, this is how sociologist Fran Tonkiss defined urban indifference:

> It is this tension between community and solitude in the city that un-
> derpins the discussion that follows. While a language of community has
> been important for articulating various politics of difference, I suggest
> that forms of *indifference* also afford certain rights to and freedoms in
> the city. The point here is not simply to set a conception of indifference
> or solitude against one of community or identity in the city, but rather
> to think about indifference as an ethical relation between subjects – one
> premised less on the 'face-to-face' relations of community than on the
> 'side-by-side' relations of anonymity.[13]

11   See Typhoon, 'Net staande'.
12   Best, *The Stranger*, 42.
13   Tonkiss, 'The Ethics of Indifference'.

As the title of Tonkiss' article, 'The Ethics of Indifference', suggests, there may be an ethics at work that implies that everyone respects the lives and cultures of others, even if they do not associate with them or get involved with one another. When push comes to shove, the issue at stake is the right for all to live in the city. If this right exists, it can only be established when people are not subjected to processes of othering.

The urgent need for de-othering was expressed even before processes of decolonization had been realized. The problem concerned the question of how to re-establish an identity and self-conscious forms of cultural subjectivities if minds and bodies of people had been impinged on by centuries of colonial ideology. One of the pivotal thinkers for the project was Frantz Fanon (1925-1961), an Afro-French psychiatrist born in Martinique. He studied the psychopathology of colonization: the damage done to the self and to collective selves. The titles of his studies expressed as much: *Black Skin, White Masks: The Experiences of a Black Man in a White World* (1952) and *The Wretched of the Earth: A Negro Psychoanalist's Study of the Problems of Racism & Colonialism in the World Today* (1961). The first addressed the socio-psychological effects of colonialism and the processes of objectification of people of different skin colour. In the second study, Fanon argued that this was not just a concern for the colonized but also the colonizers – in this case, Europeans.

De-othering was also part of the struggles of equal cultural interaction and the fight for identities and rights in the 1960s. In this context, Malcolm X made a famous statement:

> We declare our right on this earth to be a man, to be a human being, to be respected as a human being, to be given the rights of a human being in this society, on this earth, in this day, which we intend to bring into existence *by any means necessary*.[14]

The last phrase became particularly controversial because it appeared to suggest that Malcolm X supported the use of violence in this struggle. Perhaps not surprisingly, remarks like this were distinctly less controversial in a white context, given that systemic violence against African-Americans was daily business – and remains so up until this day.

If we compare the situation of the 1960s with the current circumstances, both pivotal coincidences and differences can be traced between current forms of civil right struggles and the civil rights movement in the United States

14   Malcolm X, '(1964) Malcolm X's Speech'.

of America of the previous century. The difference can be captured by the distinction between *roots* and *routes*, a distinction that coincides with a shift from the dominance of the state to powerful networks of global urban centres. The question in the 1960s and 1970s was where people originally came from as a matter of identity, since they were living in a nation-state that did not fully respect their rights. Nowadays, the lives of many are defined by urban environments which connect them to others through networks by means of which people move and form routes. These are also lines of connection.

Essentially, current empires or nation-states are confronted with new spaces, places, borders, and flows, due to which the notions of the stranger and other come to function differently. We can specify these as new forms of *territories* (distinguishing between state, region, urban zones, cities, districts, quarters, or neighbourhoods), new forms of *borders* that define such territories, new forms of *routes* across such borders or between territories, and new forms of *networks* established by such routes. All four terms used can be marked geographically or digitally, in terms of media. In the light of these complexities, the juxtaposition of self and other, or self and stranger, can no longer be maintained on the basis of simple dichotomies.

With respect to this, geographer Edward Soja reflected on the work of French urban philosopher Henri Lefebvre (1901-1991), who argued that dichotomies rhetorically aim to avoid that people think about third possibilities. Instead of an *either/or* logic, Lefebvre and Soja argued in favour of a *both-and-also* logic.[15] In this context, international studies scholar Alpha Abebe wrote an important piece in which she expanded on a new culturo-political concept: *Afropolitanism*. The term was coined in 2005 by British-born, American-raised writer of Nigerian and Ghanaian origin, Taiye Selasi, who stated:

> They (read: we) are Afropolitans. [...] There is at least one place on the African continent to which we tie our sense of self: be it a nation-state (Ethiopia), a city (Ibadan), or an auntie's kitchen. Then there's the G8 city or two (or three) that we know like the backs of our hands, and the various institutions that know us for our famed focus. We are Afropolitans: not citizens, but Africans of the world.[16]

An important distinction is being made here, between national citizens, with all their rights, and people who belong to another kind of *polis*, one that

15   Soja, *Seeking Spatial Justice*.
16   Selasi, 'Bye-bye Barbar'.

is not based on region, let alone territory, but consists rather of a network of connections. This is how Abebe consequently describes the situation in more detail:

> Diasporas and other transnational communities have become particularly useful case studies for scholars interested in stretching and challenging mainstream conceptions of citizenship. It is now widely accepted that for many people around the world, physical location and formal legal citizenship may not be the most salient forms of social, political or economic affiliation. As the process of globalization continues to expand, more and more people find themselves in one place, while their lives are structured and oriented by connections to one or several other places. Some of these 'places' are other nation states, such as an ancestral country of origin. However, many such 'places' exist extraterritorially as abstract yet powerful expressions of identity, community, and belonging.[17]

Abebe is exploring new forms of citizenship in this case: new forms of rights, driven by a logic of affiliation that is more defined by routes than roots, in a dynamic of transnationalism, of regions connecting, or of capital cities, and yet other urban centres operating through a logical network.

In this context, literary and urban scholar Jeremy Tambling argued that capital cities in particular have developed:

> complex relations to the country they represent: they embody its nationalism, but since they attract disparate populations, and immigration – cities are full of people who are the first generation to live there – they produce a plurality threatening to undo all nationalism.[18]

Urban conglomerations like Lagos, Cairo, Paris, Cape Town, Brussels, New Delhi, or London are no longer simple representations of a nation-state, because they have become too multicultural.

In these circumstances, people's cultural or political identities may still be marked by a dynamic between urban centres and suburbs, so-called *banlieues*. With regard to this dynamic, Lefebvre posed the question who has the right to the city, referring not only to the city as a space appropriated by commercial forces, but also a city that had separated the centre of administration or the political centre from the people inhabiting the

---

17   Abebe, 'Afropolitanism'.
18   Tambling, 'Prologue', 2.

city.[19] People should not be locked up in socially depressing, isolated urban outskirts, that is. Instead, they should have the right to determine their own lives in a city that enables equal chances and prospects. It is no coincidence that whenever people stand up against forms of injustice, their protests will ultimately take place in, and address the city centres. This is where they want to express and claim their rights.

To make matters even more complex, the identity of selves in urban global nodes and networks has acquired another quality and status in the context of situations that have changed from diversity to *superdiversity*.[20] Nowadays, peoples from more than hundred different cultures live together in urban centres, the Netherlands being only one example thereof. The positive indifference described by Tonkiss would again be at stake as an ethic in all the interactions involved. It concerns a mode of behaviour that does not demand that all people integrate, but that they interact on the basis of their free will.

Superdiversity also invites a specific problem, namely how people can understand one another across cultural differences. This will be the topic of the next chapter. Its question will be: if there are plenty of different cultural selves, are they all equally comparable and can everything they embody be translated – or are there principal incompatibilities?

The song that opened this part of the chapter may illustrate both the theme of this chapter and the following one. The Dutch title of the song could not be more simple: 'We zijn er.' Yet its simplicity is exactly what makes it so hard to translate; it may even be 'untranslatable'. The adverb 'er' in the phrase 'We zijn er' only becomes meaningful in the context of a sentence. It can mean 'We are here' or 'We have arrived', as a matter of relief or confirmation. Depending on the emphasis, it may mean 'We *are* here', implying that people are here to stay. From this perspective, the song is about the history of Africans who were enslaved and transported to Surinam. Many of their descendants came to settle in the Netherlands, especially in the context of Surinam's independence in 1975. They arrived *there*, to stay *here*. Finally, the phrase can even mean: 'We zijn *er*' when the verb is a copula and the 'er' a predicate. In that case, people are compared to an indistinctive linguistic unity. The issue of untranslatability is not simply a linguistic matter here, but also raises the question whether people from different cultures can truly understand each other.

19   Lefebvre, *Writings on Cities* (originally published in French in 1968).
20   Vertovec, 'Super-diversity and Its Implications'.

9. Self and Other: In-comparability

9.1. Translation: What is needed to *understand* other cultures?

Ne me quitte pas
Il faut oublier
Tout peut s'oublier
Qui s'enfuit déjà
Oublier le temps
Des malentendus
Et le temps perdu
À savoir comment
Oublier ces heures
Qui tuaient parfois
À coups de pourquoi
Le cœur du bonheur
Ne me quitte pas
Ne me quitte pas
Ne me quitte pas
Ne me quitte pas

'Ne me quitte pas' by Nina Simone (1965)[1]

This chapter will deal with why translation may imply basic forms of understanding and misunderstanding as soon as people start to interact culturally. In the context of both translation and cultural interaction, we will also be defining the pivotal difference between understanding and communication. We do so by looking at the famous comic by Hergé, *Tintin*, and by introducing a work by South African authors Antjie Krog, Nosisi Mpolweni, and Kopano Ratele, *There Was This Goat: Investigating the Truth Commission Testimony of Notrose Nobomvu Konile* (2009).

An iconic movie that thematizes understanding and misunderstanding as well as the difficulties of communicating across cultures is the film LOST IN TRANSLATION (2003, directed by Sofia Coppola), starring comedian Bill Murray and actress Scarlett Johansson. The protagonist is an American named Bob Harris, a middle-aged successful actor who poses for a Japanese whiskey commercial. However, he does not speak the language and

---

1   Simone, 'Ne me quitte pas'.

understands nothing of what he is being told to do. Not too surprisingly, he does understand an American scholar whom he meets in the hotel and the two experience a strange kind of remote romance in Tokyo. Though generally highly rated in the West, the movie was received differently in Asia and Japan. In this respect, the movie showcases the problem of intercultural communication and understanding and embodies the respective challenges that arise. For instance, film scholar Homay King remarked that the movie does not sufficiently:

> clarify that its real subject is not Tokyo itself, but Western perceptions of Tokyo. [...] When Japan appears superficial, inappropriately erotic, or unintelligible, we are never completely sure whether this vision belongs to Coppola, to her characters, or simply to a Hollywood cinematic imaginary.[2]

The quote illustrates that the movie did not just thematize miscommunication, but also provoked forms of misunderstandings, interculturally speaking. The distinction between understanding and communication is pivotal here – and translations of a famous comic by a Belgian author can help to clarify this distinction.

Georges Remi (1907-1983) wrote under the pen name Hergé and published 24 albums featuring the protagonist Tintin. They were amongst the most popular comics in Europe, translated into more than 70 languages, with 200 million copies sold, and with most albums adapted for radio, television, theatre, and film. One example is *The Crab with the Golden Claws*, originally from 1943, which was translated for the Egyptian market in 1979. For this translation, the order of the images had to be reversed, since Arabic is read from right to left (also valuable information for any multinational advertisement production). Reading from left to right may seem the same as reading from right to left, as if the two are mirrored. Yet the two forms also embody different *styles*. Styles do not just concern different ways of ordering, they also concern an attitude, a distinct aesthetic, and a way of behaving. Additionally, there were changes made to the content, because some expressions were culturally sensitive. For instance, 'By the beard of the prophet, I will get you this time' was changed into 'You won't escape, I'll get you this time.' In the Egyptian context, then, the album came to communicate something different.

As for the content, the same album makes clear how things can be untranslatable due to misunderstanding. For instance, in the album's USA

2   King, 'Lost in Translation'.

version, Captain Haddock's alcoholism had to be toned down, which to a French audience may sound unnecessary. More tellingly, black characters were to be replaced in the album, or overt racism had to be softened into tacit racism. Hergé himself noted sarcastically: 'What the American editor wanted was the following: No blacks. Neither good blacks nor bad blacks. Because blacks are neither good nor bad: they don't exist (as everyone knows, in the USA).'[3] Accordingly, Hergé replaced the African-American characters by characters he called 'of an indeterminate race' but who by and large follow the stereotypes of Eastern European or Middle Eastern ones.[4] Meanwhile, Hergé appeared to be blind to the colonialism, racism, sexism, and orientalism that characterized his albums.

If we extend our analysis in terms of communication and understanding, the former connotes what we are able to share – also the etymological root of 'communication'. In terms of cultural interactions, we can communicate what we are able to share. To understand indicates something else, for its etymological root shows that it concerns an *in-between*; the 'under' of 'understand' resembles the 'inter' in 'interest'. Accordingly, if people understand something, this means that they are somewhere in the middle of things. As a result, they can understand things that they do *not* share with others. They can even understand a radically different position without being able to communicate it.

Because communication and understanding are distinct from one another, mismatches may occur, for example, when people think they have communicated something, but their target audience has understood them differently. Such possible mismatches have only multiplied now that 'to communicate' has often acquired the meaning of 'sending things out', as when people say: 'I have communicated this many times now.' They imply that they did send messages, but did not sufficiently wonder or check whether all information was *shared*.

In Hergé's works many things are both being sent out and shared, though the question is, what does the sharing mean? Hergé's portrayals of basically all thinkable 'others' – from Congolese, to Russians, Eastern Europeans, Arabs, Chinese, to Native Americans – strengthen the viewpoint that non-Western Europeans are animal-like, childlike, unintelligent, or fantasy characters. Hergé's knowledge of American racism did not mean he was innocent himself, then, as is shown in his second album, *Tintin in the Congo*. Written in the 1920s, the album depicted Congo as a colony of Belgium,

3   Hergé quoted in Assouline, *Hergé*, 160.
4   Ibid.

and the images tell as much. Even when the album was adapted in 1946 because of a change in political circumstances, neither racism nor the colonial attitude had ceased to protrude. It led a Congolese citizen, Bienvenu Mbutu Mondondo, to take the book to court, claiming that it promoted colonialist propaganda and amounted to racism and xenophobia. The case was investigated by a court in Brussels from 2007 to 2011; the court ended up deciding that the maker had not intended to incite racial hatred.

The case is a poignant example of how intentions in intercultural communication should always be assessed in relation to what receivers feel or understand, are influenced by, or are hurt by. The issue is paramount because there have been a number of people and philosophers who are steadfastly convinced that people can come to a shared universal understanding, if only they would try. The early decades of the nineteenth century, for instance, witnessed a growing international circulation and reception of literary works from different cultures in Europe. It inspired Johan Wolfgang Goethe (1749-1832) to consider works of literature from different cultures as a matter of *Weltliteratur*, in terms of a universal understanding.

In contrast, French philologist and philosopher Barbara Cassin produced the *Vocabulaire européen des philosophies: Dictionaires des intraduisibles* (2004), translated in English as the *Dictionary of Untranslatables: A Philosophical Lexicon* (2014). In an interview she made her position very clear:

> I have two enemies: the Heideggerian way of thinking, which roots language in nation and race or strain, and which imagines that some languages are better than others as they are nearer to, let us say, the language of Being – so Greek and German, more Greek than Greek. This hierarchy of tongues and ontological nationalism is what I didn't want. [...] And the other enemy was analytic philosophy, done badly in France, which says, for example, that we all think the same, that there is no problem of tongues, of languages, and no problem of time (Aristotle could very well be my colleague at Oxford), that the universal is universal and we are all human. So I didn't believe in this either, and I don't like the effects it has.[5]

It may be evident that Cassin is looking for an in-between position. She wants to understand differences, not explain them away by means of hierarchies or universal understanding. A telling example of the distinction that Cassin is talking about is the difference between *people/peuple/pueblo/popolo* and *Volk/volk*. The first indicates a populace, a body of citizens, a multitude. The

5   Walkowitz, 'Translating the Untranslatable.

second indicates a multitude also but in the sense of a tribe, an army (troop). The former aligns with a state or republic, the latter connotes the existence of a community or nation. The difference between the two concepts and their consequent connotations does not mean that people should not try to translate them. In fact, this difference promotes constant attempts to translate.

The untranslatable nature of concepts has political implications, as was argued by literary theorist Emily Apter in *Against World Literature: On the Politics of Untranslatability* (2013). The title makes clear that Apter is arguing against the Goethean universality of understanding. She is also arguing against the hegemony of English in the context of the different c/ Cultures that shape life on this planet. Apter contends there is a need for extensive processes of translation that do justice to the original languages of people. Philosopher Homi Bhabha argued similarly when addressing cultural translation, which would involve respect for both the cultural source and the culture for which the translation was produced. According to Bhabha, our focus should lie on the translator, as opposed to the translation. Furthermore, people might want to be sensitive to mixed forms of languages and cultures, in terms of hybridity. The importance of this approach has increased in the context of migration and material movements, in the crossing of borders or border zones that exist as separate third spaces.

Translation is not simply a matter of equating one meaning with another, then, especially not in the realm of cultural understanding. If we look at the subtitle of this book, *Conflict and Cooperation*, conflicts may be the result of people not understanding one another fully when different cultures interact. Cultures embody different styles and, equally fundamentally, different *worlds*. This implies political disparity, as opposed to universality or universal understanding. As for cooperation: cultural interaction implies that human beings need relentless attempts to translate, both in order to see what they are able to share, in terms of communication, and to know and feel what they are able to understand. Here, translation does not need to be a complete success. Yet the untranslatable may still provoke the continuing attempt.

Despite the harmonious fantasies of all people coming to understand one another in the end, we have to take seriously that research suggests that there is more miscommunication than fruitful communication. Phrased differently, seemingly successful communication may be coincidental. This holds not only for cultural interactions, but also applies to people who belong to the same culture. It even holds for families, friends, and partners.

We began this part of the chapter with a famous song by French-Belgian singer Jacques Brel (1929-1978), 'Ne me quitte pas', covered by Nina Simone (1933-2003). Simone could well have sung it in English, but she chose not to. One reason may have been that the original in French expresses scenarios that dissipate in English. Jamie J. Brunson, for instance, translated the opening line as: 'Please don't leave me.' The 'please' is added to not compromise the rhythm, since French has two words to express a negation: *ne ... pas*. This introduces the need for adding a word. Still, in the French original 'please' is not uttered at all. Then, French *quitter* has several meanings: to go away, leave, leave behind, separate, stop. The last meaning is still captured by the English 'to quit'. The English translation 'don't leave me' is in this context a weak translation in terms of connotations.

It may be obvious that translations can be compared, also in terms of adequacy. In the next part of this chapter, we will be dealing with the aspect of *comparing* cultures. Here the element of adequacy takes on a different meaning.

9.2.   Does cross-cultural understanding have its limits?

Stanley, *A Gamelan Orchestra Playing at a Cremation Ceremony on Kuta Beach, Bali* (2011)[6]

6   Stanley, *A Gamelan Orchestra*.

If scholars want to compare things, they need to have something on which to base their comparison. If we compare two people, for instance, we need to know what we are comparing: height, health, eye colour, etc. Academically, the comparison of the study of cultures in Europe originates from the nineteenth century, and was initiated in the context of colonial empires. Implicitly or explicitly, the academic comparison between cultures was often based on scales of civilization (cf. Chapter 5). These were the times of the establishment of ethnological museums that intended to grasp the 'other', or to make the strange both exotic and nearby. The so-called Ethnographic Museum in Leiden is one example thereof. Initially, it consisted of a private collection with a strong focus on Japan: 'The Collection Von Siebold' was officially opened in 1837. Then it became 'The Kingdom's Ethnographic Museum' in 1864. Its name changed to 'Kingdom's Museum for the Study of Nations' in 1935. It became part recently, in conjunction with three other museums, of the 'National Museum for World Cultures'. The term 'world cultures' suggests that this museum presents the different cultures of the world, and supposedly does so equitably. However, ethnography involves the description of peoples, which implies that someone claims to be in the position from which to study them. The Dutch term *volkenkunde* tells as much, for it connotes the knowledge of nations – and in the previous chapter we discussed the difference between 'people' and '*volk*'.

The Leiden Ethnographic Museum is a paradigm of how the discipline of anthropology – the study of how human beings organize their modes of living within specific environments – was prefigured in collections, which then turned into museums. Or, to a large extent, anthropology started in museums rather than in universities. An important function of museums was to educate the public. This implied a general dissemination of discourse: a collective sharing of ways of speaking about other peoples and their cultures. Up until today, museums use a rhetoric of exhibiting: they present material and frame narratives in such a way as to convey particular meanings. That is: museums translate the cultures that they exhibit for their visitors by means of suggesting that, as museums, they make it possible to compare different cultures.

Just because colonial empires have collapsed, this does not mean that the comparison has vanished. Currently, comparison is simply driven by other forms of empire: the most notorious possibly being that of international business. In this context, one of the most well-known models of comparison was established by Geert Hofstede, an organizational psychologist who worked in the late 1960s with the USA-based international corporation IBM (International Business Machines Corp). IBM had factories and partners in different regions and countries, which led to considerable challenges in communication and understanding. Trying to understand cultures by comparing them, Hofstede decided to compare them on the basis of six dimensions:

power distance
individualism – collectivism
femininity – masculinity
uncertainty avoidance
long-term orientation – short-term orientation
indulgence – restraint[7]

The website presenting work that was further developed in collaboration with Gert Jan Hofstede (a biologist originally, and expert on the evolution of cultures) describes culture as follows:

Do we need to bother about culture? Every visitor of this site has her or his unique personality, history, and interest. At the same time, we share our human nature. We are group animals. We use language and empathy, and practice collaboration and inter-group competition. The unwritten rules of how we do these things differ from one human group to another. 'Culture' is how we call these unwritten rules about how to be a good member of the group.[8]

There are political, economic, religious, and gender aspects present in the above quotation. Yet the definition of culture is, again, rather general, or unspecified, especially if it concerns the issue whether one is a 'good member'. Yet the dimensions that made Hofstede's comparison possible were very specific and had a considerable scholarly impact, although they were fiercely criticized as well.

Hofstede's ideas were and still are used, for instance, by a company called Hofstede Insights, which specializes in helping businesses to act interculturally. The definition of culture given on their website is 'the collective mental programming of the human mind which distinguishes one group of people from another'.[9] On their site, the dimensions are defined as follows:

7   The most recent publication, and best seller, is Hofstede, Hofstede and Minkov, *Cultures and Organizations*.
8   Hofstede and Hofstede, 'Geert Hofstede and Gert Jan Hofstede on Culture'.
9   Hofstede Insights, 'Compare Countries'.

Power distance
People in societies that exhibit a large degree of Power Distance accept a hierarchical order in which everybody has a place that needs no further justification. In societies with low Power Distance, people strive to equalise the distribution of power and demand justification for inequalities of power.[10]

So, if Malaysia scores 100 and Austria 11, this means that people in Malaysia accept large discrepancies of power, whereas in Austria people do not.[11]

Individualism – collectivism
The high side of this dimension, called individualism, can be defined as a preference for a loosely-knit social framework in which individuals are expected to care only for themselves and their immediate families. Its opposite, collectivism, represents a preference for a tightly-knit framework in society in which individuals can expect their relatives or members of a particular in-group to look after them in exchange for unquestioning loyalty.[12]

If the United States scores 91 and Guatemala 6, this means that individualism is highly valued in the United States (Cf. Chapter 5), whereas in Guatemala much less so. Alternatively, one could also conclude that the collective is way more important in Guatemala. Note, meanwhile, that the way things are graded in this model is itself culturally determined, for why would individualism score high and collectivism low? One could of course argue that the model could equally well have been graded the other way around. But then again, it isn't. The same holds for the following pair:

Femininity – masculinity
The Masculinity side of this dimension represents a preference in society for achievement, heroism, assertiveness and material rewards for success. Society at large is more competitive. Its opposite, femininity, stands for a preference for cooperation, modesty, caring for the weak and quality of life. Society at large is more consensus-oriented.[13]

---

10   All following definitions are taken from the Hofstede Insights website as an example of how Hofstede's ideas started to travel. They are all close to how Hofstede himself developed his definitions. See Hofstede Insights, 'National Culture'.

11   Hofstede Insights, 'Compare Countries'.

12   Ibid.

13   Ibid.

The gendered or biased definition of this dimension isn't the issue for now – although it certainly is a highly controversial issue. Yet, if we use it, it appears that Japan's score of 95 is markedly different from Sweden: with a score of 5, the former would be more strongly masculine, the latter more strongly feminine.

Uncertainty avoidance
The Uncertainty Avoidance dimension expresses the degree to which the members of a society feel uncomfortable with uncertainty and ambiguity. The fundamental issue here is how a society deals with the fact that the future can never be known: should we try to control the future or just let it happen? Countries exhibiting strong UAI [Uncertainty Avoidance Index] maintain rigid codes of belief and behaviour and are intolerant of unorthodox behaviour and ideas. Weak UAI societies maintain a more relaxed attitude in which practice counts more than principles.[14]

In Greek culture, with a score of 100, people tend to consider the future as something radically uncertain or different, which is why they want to stick to the way things are. In Singapore, with a score of 8, people appear to deal with the future flexibly, as a matter of practice.

Long-term orientation – short-term orientation
Societies that score low on this dimension, for instance prefer to maintain time-honoured traditions and norms while they view societal change with suspicion. Those with a culture which scores high, on the other hand, take a more pragmatic approach: they encourage thrift and efforts in modern education as a way to prepare for the future.[15]

China scoring 118 and Ghana 4, shows a significant difference, which implies that Chinese culture easily adapts to new circumstances whereas Ghanese culture wants to preserve old traditions.

Indulgence – restraint
Indulgence stands for a society that allows relatively free gratification of basic and natural human drives related to enjoying life and having fun. Restraint stands for a society that suppresses gratification of needs and regulates it by means of strict social norms.[16]

14   Ibid.
15   Ibid.
16   Ibid.

Here, Ghana scores relatively high, with 72, and China relatively low, with 24, which implies that Ghanaian culture is way more open to a variety of practices and behaviours than Chinese culture. Ghanaian culture is also slightly more indulgent, here, than the Netherlands, which scores 68, and much more than Russian culture that with 20 scores lower than Chinese culture.

Recently, Erin Meyer published *The Culture Map: Breaking Through the Invisible Boundaries of Global Business* (2014) in which she developed another model, based on eight scales. She distinguished aspects of doing business on the basis of the following parameters:

Communicating: explicit vs. implicit
Evaluating: direct negative feedback vs. indirect negative feedback
Persuading: deductive vs. inductive
Leading: egalitarian vs. hierarchical
Deciding: consensual vs. top down
Trusting: task vs. relationship
Disagreeing: confrontational vs. avoid confrontation
Scheduling: structured vs. flexible

When using Meyer's model for comparing the Netherlands to Poland and Ukraine, for instance, the following is the result: Dutch people tend to strive for consensus in processes of decision making, whereas the Polish will be satisfied with someone at the top deciding. Yet when it concerns moments of conflict, both the Dutch and the Polish tend to solve problems by being confrontational, read: 'blunt'. This comparison may highlight that comparisons are always relative, depending on the parameters being compared. Comparing either Dutch people, Polish or Ukrainians with Tanzanian and Indonesian people will lead to different results.

In the current situation, whether with the Hofstedes or Meyer, the comparative impulse is predominantly motivated by international 'organizations', corporations, business networks, and trade. As was also the case in the colonial context, the question is to what purpose a cultural comparison is made. Is it in order to enhance understanding and sensibility, or to maximize efficiency and profit? Of course, the two do not exclude each other, but they do not completely coincide either. Especially in the context of growing cultural interaction, the need to study differences and coincidences between cultures may be evident, if only to see whether change is possible, or to explain how affairs have changed.

As for change, one paradigmatic case is Hong Kong, considering that it was under British rule for almost 150 years. Did this have an impact on the cultural predisposition of people towards mainland China? On the basis of Hofstede's model, we do see some marginal changes – although these can also exist as regional differences within China. Two of them are striking: people in Hong Kong have become more individualistic, and have become distinctly more attached to traditions in terms of long-term orientation, for instance the tradition of how to organize themselves politically.

Since comparing cultures on the basis of dimensions or scales relates to translation and understanding, the models have a heuristic capacity. With heuristics we indicate instruments, ways, modes to search or look for information. Using any of the instruments dealt with above, helps us to search, then; not to find essences. We can only hope that in doing so, we can compare and perhaps interact more productively, carefully, or sensibly, as the simple application of these models raises considerable problems. One immediate objection is that we may essentialize notions of culture, of masculinity and femininity, or deal with traits that can easily foster stereotypical undertones. The strong emphasis on communication in the model of Meyer may blur the complexity of large-scale cultural interactions. Also, both models may have a deceiving explanatory power. Once we have defined things in a certain way, the framework becomes visible everywhere we look, or the very description of a culture suggests that we know it, without having any idea how this culture became what it is.

Last but not least, the strong emphasis on national cultures may be inadequate when we consider how many nation-states are fairly new and forced constructions. Secondly, what does comparison do in deeply multi-cultural societies or federations? Can the models do justice to the tension between national and transnational identity or to the dynamic of multiple diasporas? (cf. Chapter 8). The Hofstede Insights website offers clear scales, for example, of South Africa. The question remains how such homogeneity is possible for a deeply multicultural society.

The massive cultural differences in South Africa, also in terms of un-derstanding each other across cultures, were at the centre of a 2009 study by Antjie Krog, Nosisi Mpowlweni, and Kopano Ratele: *There Was This Goat: Investigating the Truth Commission Testimony of Notrose Nobomvu Konile*. The book's main topic was the testimony of one of the women who had spoken in front of the Truth and Reconciliation Commission (TRC). This commission was active from 1995 to 2000 and was implemented as a search for restorative justice in South Africa after Apartheid. The intention of the Commission was to 'heal the past' and to work towards collective understanding, communication, and justice. One of the interviewees was Notrose Nobomvu Konile, the mother of a seventeen-year-old young man who had been lured into a trap by the South African secret service and had been executed in Gugulethu township on the morning of 3 March 1986. His mother came to tell her story about what had happened.

Now, there are eleven official South African languages: Afrikaans, English, Ndbele, Northern Soto, Sotho, Swazi, Tsonga, Tswana, Venda, Xhosa, and Zulu. Consequently:

> Witnesses at TRC hearings were able to give testimony in their home language. Translators and transcribers worked in most of South Africa's 11 official languages plus Polish. As a result, spelling errors (particularly of names) occur. There may also be incorrect transcription or translation in places. There are also many instances where a response was inaudible and gaps appear in the transcription.[17]

Apparently, the issue was, again, whether translation was simply a matter of communication or whether it related to the collision of worlds and to the possibility to understand these worlds from different sides. Studying the testimony of the mother for the TRC, the three authors noticed that it had become an incoherent text in translation. The mother seemed to ramble on about a goat, for instance, which had nothing to do with the case. Yet the text became completely comprehensible if a dream of the mother, in which a goat had acted as a premonition of her son's death, was taken seriously. In studying her text, the scholars uncovered:

> the flaws in the interpretation of Konile's TRC testimony, but also discovered how the vastly diverse experiences and histories of South Africans continue to complicate understanding and the ability of South Africans to hear one another.[18]

The 'ability to hear one another' is explicitly a matter of understanding here, rather than one of communication. And in the context of centuries of asymmetrical interaction, 'diverse experiences and histories' involve a variety of languages and cultures. Both the model of Hofstede and that of Meyer will be of limited value when dealing with such complexities.

---

17   This is what the website of the TRC tells us (Truth and Reconciliation Committee, 'Human Rights Violations').
18   Basson, 'The Dream Truths of Notrose Konile'.

We started this chapter with Gamelan music from the island of Bali, in Indonesia. Perhaps music is most paradigmatic in illustrating why cultural comparison has distinct and insurmountable limits. There is little to be gained from comparing Gamelan music to, for instance, European classical music. More fundamentally, music is untranslatable. The question as to whether music communicates anything is also of relevance. Without a doubt, though, music embodies pivotal modes of understanding. Music does not so much raise the question how people listen to music, but rather what they hear while listening. Perhaps music is the best starting point for dealing with other cultures in terms of respect and understanding. Everything starts with listening and trying to hear the resonances in question in any message.

In the next chapter we will listen to different things, as we consider how cultures cope with abilities and inabilities. How do cultures actually distinguish between abilities and inabilities? And how can we study the processes of cultural interactions in relation to abilities?

10. Culture and Dis-abled Selves: Normality

Beethoven, *Symphonie nr 9, Partiturerstausgabe* (1826)[1]

10.1. How is disability historically and culturally determined?

In the previous chapters we dealt with collectives in terms of culture as a form-of-life and related it to notions such as nation-state, world, society,

1 Beethoven, *Symphonie nr 9*.

civilization, and community. We proceeded to investigate the way in which culture relates to the constitution of selves by looking at forms of identity, affiliation, and possibilities or impossibilities of mutual understanding. In the coming three chapters, we will look at certain standards by means of which cultural selves are measured, in terms of normality, animality, and artificiality.

The first part of this chapter focuses on how cultures have been determining human selves in terms of (dis)abilities and how human selves have been organized by means of norms and normality with the advent of modernity. In both cases, we will ask what affordances are offered by cultures or to selves who deviate from the norm(al) – and we will be defining the term 'affordance'.[2] However, before we set off, we have to notice that the very term 'disability' isn't universal across cultures and that it may therefore be inadequate. In fact, as we will realize in the second part, the term 'disability' is a modern one. As a modern notion, the question is again whether the term is helpful or whether it may be harmful. The famous Mexican artist Frida Kahlo is one example that gives food for thought. She suffered from polio at the age of six and recovered, but was left with a limp. At the age of fifteen she had a disastrous accident in a bus that collided with a tramcar, which fractured her spine and pelvis and left her in pain and partly immobile for the rest of her life. The effect was that several scholars and critics looked at her life and especially artistic work in terms of her disability. The simple question is: should the work of hosts of other artists be considered in the light of their *not* suffering from something, then?

Not only did the very term 'disability' not exist as such in previous periods and a variety of cultures, the entire conceptualization of what it means to be disabled differed substantially. For instance, tradition has it that one of the most famous poets in the history of the West, the classical Greek poet Homer, was blind. Yet this blindness was not a hindrance, but in fact opened up another potential. Another example: the Netflix series VIKINGS had the figure of the Seer, the Oracle of Kattegat. His inability to see, in the physical world, strengthened his capacity of having a wider reaching inner eye. The very same series, moreover, introduces Ivar Ragnarsson, or Ivar the Boneless, as a main character, who is based on a real historical character, Ívarr hinn Beinlausi. Historically it is uncertain whether he was lame, had no legs, or had legs but was impotent. Whatever the case, it did not stop

---

2   The analysis of disabilities in terms of affordances was proposed by Andries Hiskes in a research project entitled 'Against Staring: Disability and Its Affective Affordances – Deformity, Decay, Disruption, Distortion'. See Van Ertvelde and Hiskes, 'Disability and Academia'.

him from becoming one of the great and notoriously feared Viking leaders. In fact, if we take the Middle Ages as a frame of reference, there may have been more people with some sort of, what would now be called, disability than people who had none. Forms of impairment were so common that people did not recognize them as a matter of disability.

Then there is the question of what counts as disability and what does not. The previous chapter, for instance, dealt with the South African Truth and Reconciliation Committee and we discussed the ability to translate something so simple and yet complex as a dream. There were also a lot of people attending the committee, moreover, who suffered from a trauma, which literally means 'wound'. In the context of trauma studies, trauma is a lasting wound that is difficult or impossible to heal. Trauma may disable peoples' capacity to express what happened to them, or to express themselves fully. So, if trauma is generally not considered a matter of disability, there are good reasons to at least consider trauma as a matter of inability. Then, in the South African context, after the abolition of Apartheid, this did not mean that all people were equal in their ability to express themselves. Many had been framed by a system that marked them as incapable of expressing themselves, and this had lasting effects.

Tellingly, various scholars speak of a sociocultural 'Apartheid' in the force fields of abilities and disabilities. Transposing the term 'Apartheid' to this field implies that disabled people of different kinds are considered to be second-class citizens, who live in their environment but cannot fully participate in society at large. Such an analysis depends on the dominant models that have steered modern thinking about disability since the nineteenth century: the medical model and the economic model, both of which consider disabilities in terms of *functional limitations*, and the sociopolitical model, which considers disabled people in terms of them being a (discriminated) *minority*.

In dealing with culture as a form-of-life, another possibility arises, which was also developed in the field of disability studies. This is how Anne Waldschmidt defined the cultural model of disability:

[A] cultural model of disability should regard neither disability nor impairment as clear-cut categories of pathological classification that automatically, in the form of a causal link, result in social discrimination. Rather, this model considers impairment, disability *and* normality as effects generated by academic knowledge, mass media, and everyday discourses.[3]

3   Waldschmidt, 'Disability Goes Cultural', 24.

The cultural aspect implies, then, that we look at the definition within a given culture of what counts as normal, or what is considered to be the norm. for Waldschmidt, disability or impairment is 'not a natural fact but a naturalized difference'. This naturalization of what is actually symbolically constructed can then be critically weighed to open up new modes of dealing with disability.[4]

Still, as it is, and especially since the nineteenth century, disabled people have either been marginalized, considered as a matter of fascination, or their disability has prompted problems of representation. One poignant example is the way in which one of the most famous disabled characters in European history has been represented: Oedipus. The nineteenth-century painting below shows him with his daughter, Antigone, leading him out of Thebes because of the shame placed on Oedipus.

The story has it that without his being aware of it, Oedipus has killed his own father and married his mother. This had been predicted when he was born, which led his father and mother to cut the tendons in his feet, abandoning him in the fields as food for wild animals. *Oedipus* does not mean

Jalabert, *Oedipus and Antigone* (1842)[5]

4   Ibid, 25.
5   Jalabert, *Oedipus and Antigone*.

'swollen foot' for nothing. The little boy was discovered, though, brought to another court where he was raised, and history took its predicted course. Still, he could not walk without support, a feature that is almost always only hinted at by Oedipus' carrying a staff. This fact puzzled classicist Claire Catenaccio, who considered it strange that decades of modern study did not pay attention to Oedipus' impairment:

> relatively little attention has been paid to the wounded feet of the king as a repository of poetic meaning for the play as a whole. Why literary critics have shown so little interest in the titular theme of 'King Swollen-Foot' is a riddle indeed.[6]

One answer to this riddle is that impairments tend to make people feel uncomfortable.

Dutch history offers an example of this. When the Dutch had broken free, in the second half of the sixteenth century, from what they considered a tyrannical regime, they sought historical justification. They found it by conjuring up a myth based on a description by the Roman author Tacitus in *Histories, Book IV* of a rebellion. It relates the story of Claudius Civilis, the leader of a revolt against the Romans in the Low Countries and Germany

Rembrandt, *The Conspiracy of the Batavians under Claudius Civilis* (1661-1662)[7]

6 Catenaccio, 'Oedipus Tyrannus', 102.
7 Rembrandt, *The Conspiracy of the Batavians under Claudius Civilis.*

around 69-70 ACE. Claudius was turned into a heroic freedom fighter, and as such he was central to a painting by Rembrandt. Yet Claudius Civilis, aka Gaius Julius, was missing one eye (as was the case with many soldiers), which meant that most paintings only showed one side of his face, the side with the functioning eye. Rembrandt, however, decided not to follow this tradition; he portrayed him full face.

The painting from 1662 was intended to be a central piece in the newly built Amsterdam City Hall (currently the Royal Palace). It was there for a couple of months, then it was taken down.[8] The fact that the painting was rejected may have been a matter of taste; it may also have been because the painting made people feel uncomfortable.

If one considers the term 'disability' to be inadequate, the issue becomes what it means to think about people with any form of impairment in terms of abilities and capabilities. A paradigmatic case in this context is that before North America had been colonized by Europeans, many different peoples lived there with, on estimate, 2500 languages. People could still communicate with one another by means of a sign language. Since this was understandable to deaf people as well, they were not considered a separate entity.

Now, if differing abilities need not be exceptional for a (very) long time even though they might cause unease, the question is: when, where, and why did *ableism* start? Ableism connotes something similar to racism or speciesism, namely an ideologically underpinned looking down on those who are less able than others. We will answer this question in the next part of the chapter.

The musical epigraph to this part is a famous piece by a strongly impaired man: Ludwig von Beethoven (1770-1827), one of the most famous composers of his time, and for centuries to follow. Beethoven was distinctly troubled, and not only because he became deaf at a fairly young age. Had he lived in our times, his father would have been accused of child abuse and not just because he was an alcoholic; he used his son in a similar way to how Wolfgang Amadeus Mozart's father had been moulding Mozart to become a child prodigy. Beethoven was a virtuoso at the age of seven and taken out of school at the age of eleven. His hearing started to rapidly deteriorate in his early 20s and he would suffer from what now probably would be diagnosed as a spastic colon. He may also have suffered from lead poisoning and surely

---

8   Rembrandt had to minimize it, from a massive 550 × 550 cm to 196 × 309 cm and it was sold to a Swedish trader.

had liver cirrhosis due to heavy drinking. Yet his deafness in particular made him creative in dealing with his surroundings. At some point he would place a wooden pole against the soundboard of the piano and clench the other part between his teeth so he could hear and feel the music again. He had a vast array of different hearing devices, so-called ear trumpets, that enlarged the receptacle of the ear. Despite all this, his music has generally not been framed by his 'disabilities'.

10.2.   What are the cultural affordances in disabilities?

I'm Spasticus, I'm Spasticus
I'm Spasticus Autisticus
I'm Spasticus, I'm Spasticus
I'm Spasticus Autisticus
I'm Spasticus, I'm Spasticus
I'm Spasticus Autisticus
I wibble when I piddle
Cos my middle is a riddle
I'm Spasticus, I'm Spasticus
I'm Spasticus Autisticus
I'm Spasticus, I'm Spasticus
I'm Spasticus Autisticus
I'm Spasticus, I'm Spasticus
I'm Spasticus Autisticus
I dribble when I nibble
And I quibble when I scribble
Hello to you out there in Normal Land
You may not comprehend my tale or understand
As I crawl past your window give me lucky looks
You can be my body but you'll never read my books

'Spasticus Autisticus' by Ian Dury[9]

Ian Dury – British artist, singer-songwriter, and front man of the new wave band Ian Dury and the Blockheads – made a controversial song in 1981. Born in 1942, the young Ian went swimming in waters that contained the polio virus at the age of seven. The disease was treated by having him rest in a full

9   Dury, 'Spasticus Autisticus'.

plaster cast for six weeks and this left him with a withering of the left leg, shoulder, and arm. He later trained as an artist and started making music. His single 'Sex and Drugs and Rock and Roll' was banned by the BBC for being too explicit in 1977, which did not hinder his career. It would not be the only song banned, moreover, for later he would write 'Spasticus Autisticus', a protest song against the International Year for Disabled Persons (1981), which he considered to be patronizing. The BBC found the song offensive once more, for it seemed to celebrate a derogatory term: 'spastic'.

However, Professor of Media Studies George McKay praised Dury for his ability to thematize disability in songs in a 2009 article:

> Ian Dury, that 'flaw of the jungle', produced a remarkable and sustained body of work that explored issues of disability, in both personal and social contexts, institutionalisation, and to a lesser extent the pop cultural tradition of disability. He also, with the single 'Spasticus Autisticus' (1981), produced one of the outstanding protest songs about the place of disabled people in what he called 'normal land'.[10]

McKay is referring to the central couplet in the song that goes:

> Hello to you out there in Normal Land
> You may not comprehend my tale or understand
> As I crawl past your window give me lucky looks
> You can be my body but you'll never read my books

Explicitly, the song addresses the issue of how cultures or societies define a norm, on the basis of which they can hierarchize and prioritize a society in terms of what is normal and what is not. People who consider themselves to be normal never wonder whether they are accepted. They are accepted, because they are the norm. Yet the force of such normality has its consequences for those who are not considered to be normal, as Dury emphasizes.

Though controversial in its own time, the song shows how things would start to change in the decades to come. Dury died from colorectal cancer in 2000 (although Bob Geldof erroneously declared him dead on radio in 1998). This meant that Dury was not there to witness his song being the centrepiece in the opening ceremony of the Paralympics in London in 2012. It may have been a form of poetic justice.

---

10   McKay, "'Crippled with Nerves'".

Historically, many physical or mental deficiencies have been symbolically charged. In Christianity, for instance, the devil could be traced through some sort of bodily impairment, since it was inconceivable that the devil would reside in a perfect body. At the same time, bodily traumas would be characteristic for a host of martyrs and saints. Blindness could be considered either a bad sign or some sort of blessing, depending on the particular context. If, in the eyes of faithful Christians, the reality of this world was nothing but a degenerate reality in light of the eternal life, blindness could help one to focus on a more worthy reality. All these cases or situations are forms of cultural *affordance*.

The term 'affordance' was coined by James J. Gibson in *The Senses Considered as Perceptual Systems* (1966) and it occurs in many of his essays, for instance, in *The Ecological Approach to Visual Perception* (1979):

> The affordances of the environment are what it offers the animal, what it provides or furnishes, either for good or ill. The verb to afford is found in the dictionary, the noun affordance is not. I have made it up. I mean by it something that refers to both the environment and the animal in a way that no existing term does. It implies the complementarity of the animal and the environment.[11]

Transposed to our topic, any form of deficiency, impairment, or disability is not an objective given. What matters are the affordances that are present in and allowed by a cultural or societal environment.

We can illustrate the notion of affordance with the case of the 'Elephant Man', Joseph Carey Merrick (1862-1890), who probably suffered from a severe form of Proteus syndrome.[12] This condition causes all sorts of textures in the body to grow asymmetrically – the Greek god Proteus could adopt malleable forms, hence the adjective 'protean'. Physically speaking, it may result in massive deformation. Due to his physical deformation, Merrick had an abysmal life in the so-called normal world, in which he was mocked and mistreated on the street. He decided to join a freak show that made him feel more at home. When he got robbed in Belgium, during one of his trips, however, he returned to England. He was molested, ended up in a hospital and met a doctor who had shown an early interest in him. This Dr. Treves from thereon took care of him, under the condition that Merrick became a spectacle for the rich and highly educated. In each circumstance, then,

---

11   Gibson, *The Ecological Approach to Visual Perception*, 127.
12   The case is analyzed in Hiskes, 'Drawn to Deviance'.

Merrick found possibilities and limits in what was offered to him and what he could do as a consequence thereof.

It was a sign of the times that it was a doctor who took care of Merrick. Over the course of the nineteenth century the new science of medicine, closely cooperating with governments and the judicial system, ended up reorganizing the entire fabric of society. Part of this procedure was also to define what was considered to be normal and what was not. The consequences can be traced in a study by Peter Cryle and Elizabeth Stephens, *Normality: A Critical Genealogy* (2017).[13] In accordance with the analysis of Foucault, they show how the nineteenth century witnessed processes of normalization due to techniques of dissection, numbering, statistics, measurements, anthropometrics, and the definition of types within certain categories. The authors also show that normality extends well beyond the realm of who is considered to be impaired or disabled. Their analysis of sexual practices in the twentieth century, for instance, also noted how different forms of behaviour were marked as either normal or perverse.

From the 1960s and 1970s onwards, people increasingly came to reflect critically on the force of normality, such as political scientist and disability activist Harlan Hahn, who expands on models we already discussed in the previous part of the chapter:

> Both the medical and economic definitions have relied primarily on clinical methods. Whereas the medical approach has been operationally measured by limits on major life activities, the economic orientation has been measured by restrictions on the amount or kind of work that can be performed. By contrast, the sociopolitical definition, which focuses on the interaction between the individual and the environment, can be empirically assessed by measures of visibility and labelling. Self-identification is also an important index of the relative size and political strength of disabled persons.[14]

Hahn's last sentence emphasizes that disabled people have their own political potential to establish their selves. Yet Hahn also mentions visibility and labelling, which are a matter of how, collectively speaking, discourses and practices contribute to the sociopolitical/sociocultural construction, framing, and acceptance of disabilities.

As gender specialist Susan Wendell noted in *The Rejected Body: Feminist Philosophical Reflections on Disability*, there is an inevitable interaction at

---

13   Cryle and Stephens, *Normality*.
14   Hahn, 'The Political Implications'.

work between the social and the biological, in order 'to create (or prevent)' disability's potential to fully realize itself.[15] In this context, a shift has been taking place in the last five decades, highlighted by the editors of *Disability in Different Cultures: Reflections on Local Concepts*, Brigitte Holzer, Arthur Vreede, and Gabriele Weight:

> This altered consciousness with regard to disabilities makes it possible to perceive a condition formerly held to be natural – where the disability was seen as an inborn physical state, entailing consequences viewed as inevitable – as something which can be both changed and shaped.[16]

The altered state of affairs relates to a reconsideration of affordances, and of the cultural construction of disabilities. Disabilities are not simply a natural given, neither are they societal possibilities. The affordances present in bodies and societies depend on how people shape them.

Still, things have not proven to be as simple as they have been presented here. For example, scholars have defined what is necessary to overcome the force of normality as a matter decolonization. This was implied by an edited collected from 2016: *Occupying Disability: Critical Approaches to Community, Justice, and Decolonizing Disability*. The very title suggests that modern thinking about normality – and consequentially the problem of defining others as fitting the category of some sort of disability – has been a form of colonization. The question is whether this is the case. Perhaps scholars tend to equate colonization, here, with what coincided with colonization; namely, the reorganization of societies on the basis of normalization.

In her *A Disability History of the United States*, a history of disability in North American Indigenous culture, Kim E. Nielsen mentions that disability was as such unknown to precolonial peoples.[17] In an interview, she states:

> The words that I kept running across were words like 'unwell' or 'unbalanced'. In many indigenous cultures, they didn't separate out mind, body, spirit the way that Western cultures have, and so the idea was to have an overall wellness. But I could have significant bodily differences and cognitive differences and still be considered balanced and well.[18]

15   Wendell, *The Rejected Body*, 35.
16   Holzer, Vreede and Weigt, 'Introduction', 10.
17   Nielsen, *A Disability History of the United States*.
18   Nielsen, 'Indigenous Peoples Day.'

Disabled people were not treated differently or separately in the process of the colonization of the Americas; for, as a result, they would now still be in need of decolonization. Rather, the very processes of colonization, in their connection to the nineteenth-century processes of normalization, redefined their status and the affordances offered to them.

A better concept to describe the coincidence of factors described above is *intersectionality* (cf. Chapter 5). The Indian social scientist Nilika Mehrotra described this as follows:

> In charting the history of disability rights movements (DRM) one needs to examine the rise of other similar movements in postcolonial India, especially the women's movements, environmental movements and more recently dalit movements. The social and political context which provided the background and the necessary impetus to these movements displays an interesting trajectory, points of conjunction and disjunction across the world.[19]

The Disability Rights Movement is considered to be a distinguishable thing in itself in this case, yet intrinsically connected to other battles for equality and justice. If such equality were to be realized, the people 'out there in Normal Land', as they were addressed by Ian Dury, would inevitably have to cooperate in shaping a world in which the normal is no longer the norm on the basis of which societal hierarchies are implemented and justified. The new norm would have to be one that finds an entire set of different colours, different capacities, and complexities 'normal'.

In the next chapter we will consider how the normalization of the world also implied that human culture placed human beings on a different plane from all other animals. There the question is: what if culture isn't specifically human? The more closely people have studied animals, the more they appear to have forms of culture. Should this redefine the relations people have with them, and their lifeworlds?

19   Mehrotra, 'Disability Rights Movements in India'.

11.   Culture and Animal Selves: Relationality

Ravi and Anoushka Shankar[1]

11.1.   How do tropes anthropomorphize animals, and animalize humans?

Music has been repeatedly connected to sounds made by animals in all cultures. In the Western tradition, birds have especially influenced the making of music. One of Mozart's compositions was based on the sounds of his pet sparrow: the so-called 'Sparrow Mass', or the 'Mass in C Major'.[2] In the twentieth century, the French composer Olivier Messiaen spent considerable time studying the sounds of birds in order to include them in his compositions. The tradition of Indian music reveals a more fundamental relation, however. Whereas Western music is based on the octave, a scale

---

1   For the music, see El2546, *Ravi & Anoushka Shankar*. For the photograph, see Josiehen, *Ravi Shankar with Anoushka Shankar*.
2   Mozart, 'Mass in C Major'.

of eight tones, the Indian system is based on a scale of seven: Shadja (षड्ज),
Rishabha (ऋषभ), Gandhara (गान्धार), Madhyama (मध्यम), Panchama (पंचम),
Dhaivata (धैवत), and Nishada (निषाद्), or Sa-Re-Ga-Ma-Pa-Dha-Ni. The notes
distinguished on this scale are believed to originate from the sounds of
animals: the peacock, the goat, the heron, the horse, the nightingale (of
course), but also the elephant – and tellingly, the bellowing of a cow when
her calf is separated from her: the 'Re' tone.

This chapter will focus on the issue of what it means when we take the
human self as the cultural norm, like when humans state that they have
'culture', whereas other animals do not. Note, meanwhile, that we have
shifted from using the phrase 'human beings' to the noun 'humans', here,
to avoid the unfortunate effect that humans are 'beings', and animals are
not. If we deal with both on an equal level, one question is whether we can
speak of animals having culture. If so, what does this imply for the ways
in which we think about 'cultural interactions' in terms of the relations
that connect many species? If human cultures are just one amongst many
different cultures, this at least has consequences for the planetary position
and relationality of humans.

Before we examine the question posed, we have to consider how the
very word 'culture' has operated predominantly in terms of (1) cultivation
and (2) representation in relation to animals. As for the first, we look at the
different ways in which animals are cultivated, or how they have become
the object of farming industries. As for the second, we consider the ways
in which animals appear in forms of cultural representation, for instance,
in a considerable number of Disney movies.

We go back in time when we talk about cultivation, when humans started
to keep so-called domesticated animals, from dogs to donkeys, cats to
camels, horses, chickens, pigs, cows, sheep, goats, rabbits, ducks, parrots, and
Guinea pigs. This is one form of cultivation. With the advent of modernity
something different materializes: the industrial cultivation of animals, with
cows, chickens, pigs, turkeys, and salmon perhaps as the most terrifying
examples. Yet also a specific kind of octopus is now being tried out as a
cultivated food source: 'It's not quite an octopus's garden, but researchers
at the Sisal campus of Mexico's national university, working closely with
local residents, may be about to establish the world's first commercial
octopus farm.'[3] The catchy mentioning of a famous Beatles song – 'Octopus's
Garden' – written by Richard Starkey or Ringo Starr, can confuse readers.
It is a fun song that contributes to the anthropomorphization of worlds

3   Working Gringos, 'Commercial Octopus Farming in Sisal'.

but in a sense still respects octopuses living down in the sea. In the case of industrialized octopus cultivation, however, the animals are gathered in boxes to be raised and killed, and any culture octopuses themselves might have is torn asunder to serve human food culture.

The term 'cultivation' indicates that certain cultures are being produced in the context and service of human cultures. Cultivated animals or beings can no longer be considered as an independent form-of-life, then, but rather come to be bare life. Critical scholars have considered this in terms of 'anthropocentrism' and 'speciesism', which was coined by Richard Ryder in the 1970s.[4] The first term indicates that the entire world is organized with humans at the centre, the second indicates an ideologically underpinned attitude that considers the human species as superior to all others.

The industrialization of animals is often defended by people claiming that the human populace continues to grow and needs to be fed, but the ethical, ecological, and cultural consequences of this stance have become more and more troubling. They have led to substantial misconceptions, such as when people think that farmed salmon efficiently creates more food. Still, as critics noted: 'While certain forms of aquaculture are currently sustainable, salmon are carnivorous, and feed on other fish in order to grow.'[5] The culinary preferences of humans, or rather their habits of consumption, may be questionable, then, given that enormous amounts of animals are needed to produce cultivated food for them.

As for the ethical consequences, scholars have been studying the combination of deanimalization and dehumanization. The former term indicates that animals are no longer considered to be living beings, but objects to be dealt with as efficiently as possible. Regarding those working in the meat industries, scholars have argued that their work is a matter of dehumanization since it demands that humans deal with other creatures in a purely instrumental and industrial way.[6] As for cultural interactions: if animal cultures are simply ignored or destroyed, there is no cultural interaction.

Rather few cultural representations of this industrialized animal cultivation exist, but the movie CHICKEN RUN (2000) by Aardman Studios and DreamWorks offers food for thought. The movie is also a good example of the ways in which animals in general appear in forms of cultural representation.

---

4   Ryder developed his thoughts since the beginning of the seventies. See Ryder, *The Political Animal*.

5   Gao, 'The Sustainability of Salmon Farming in BC'.

6   On this industrialization of animals, see Vugts, 'The Case against Animal Rights'. Vugts argues that giving animals rights is not a way to solve the problem.

Animals are being humanized, a literary tactic that is the antidote to the ways in which humans are sometimes animalized. The latter was evident in the colonial context and served to establish European superiority by downgrading others through infantilization, animalization tropes, and fantasies of 'sexual rescues': literary tropes, or 'topes of empire' that served to depict colonial subjects as children who needed to be disciplined, as animals to be exploited or in need of cultivation, or animal-like beings that served to fuel fantasies of aggression which were then countered by white heroes defending the honour of white women.[7]

A powerful example of the animalization of humans in terms of representation can be found in a work by American artist Art Spiegelman, in the two volumes of his graphic novel *Maus: A Survivor's Tale*. The first volume was subtitled *My Father Bleeds History* (1986), the second *And Here My Troubles Began* (1991). Spiegelman took seriously the dehumanizing images deployed by Nazis in their attempt to destroy Judaism and the Jewish people. The Nazis used animalization tropes to define those whom they wanted to destroy as plague animals, like mice or rats. Such methods were also part of the Rwandan genocide (April and July 1994), in which a group of people – the Tutsis – were defined as cockroaches. The same method was used in the third series of BLACK MIRROR (2011-2019), in an episode entitled 'Men against Fire', when the protagonist, a soldier, is sent out to erase humanoid mutants known as roaches. When his equipment falters, however, he suddenly discovers that his technological instruments had continuously visualized ordinary humans as vermin to be destroyed.

The twisted dynamic of animalizing others was taken seriously and consequently inverted by Spiegelman, who chose to address and counter the animalization of Jews by the Nazis – but also to use the force inherent in cartoons to affect people. In Spiegelman's graphic novel, Jews are depicted as mice, Nazis as cats, and the Polish people as dogs. This avoided sentimental identification with Shoah victims but also tapped into what Spiegelman called 'the lizard brain'.[8] He was referring to the oldest core of the human brain that immediately and affectively responds to what is seen or sensed without any critical reflection. This is indeed how such tropes work and why they are difficult to eradicate.

The tropes used in the relations between humans and animals can be specified as forms of metaphorization, personification, and

---

7   Shohat and Stam, *Unthinking Eurocentrism*, 156-161.
8   Web Exclusive, '"Cartoonist Lives Matter": Art Spiegelman Responds to Charlie Hebdo Attack, Power of Cartoons'

anthropomorphism. Tropes are figures of speech that provoke thought, or have a specific rhetorical effect. Metaphors work by means of an equation between two different terms, as a result of which one term comes to frame the other. If we say 'Zeus is an eagle' or 'Stalin is a wolf,' Zeus is framed as an eagle, and Stalin as a wolf. In the cases dealt with above, humans are equated and thus framed as animals. This may just as well be reversed, as when people say: 'Our cat is a tramp' or 'This virus is a serial killer.' Then, personification aims to indicate that human characteristics are given to nonhuman entities. If we say, for instance, that viruses are smart, we consider viruses as something humanlike, with a brain. Likewise, if we say that a cat smiles at us, this is a personification.

Anthropomorphism indicates that any entity is turned into something that belongs to a humanoid world. Anthropomorphism is often confused with personification, even by famous dictionaries and encyclopaedias. I take my cue from the literary scholar Barbara Johnson, who considered that the best way to understand anthropomorphism is name-giving.[9] For instance, if a dog is called 'Napoleon', this dog isn't compared to Napoleon, nor is it necessarily given human characteristics. Nevertheless, it is introduced into a human dominated world through its name – and probably also as property. Even the term 'dog' is an anthropomorphism. Every natural thing named is an anthropomorphism, something that is captured in a song by Bob Dylan called 'Man Gave Names to All the Animals'.[10]

A simple test may serve to show how all three tropes work in the case of a fairly well-known animal character who even made an appearance at the 2011 White House Correspondents' Dinner in a talk given by American president Obama: the character of Simba from THE LION KING (1994).[11] The fact that this lion has been given a name is an anthropomorphism. The fact that he is a lion cub who at some point will have to become king is another trope: apparently the lion is equated with a king, which is a metaphor. Finally, in the movie, this young lion is thinking and talking – all the while demonstrating a variety of human emotions: a matter of personification.

If we consider humans as 'caretakers of the world', this is a metaphor as well. Here, we witness a circularity of tropes. If humans invent a lion who is

9   Johnson, 'Anthropomorphism'.
10 Dylan, 'Man Gave Names to All the Animals'.
11 On the occasion of the White House Correspondents' Dinner in 2011, Obama revealed his 'birth certificate' – a clip from THE LION KING showing the birth of Simba – to then make explicit to the people from Fox News that this was a joke, and to make fun of Donald Trump, who had publicly doubted whether Obama was born a US citizen. See CNN, *Watch Obama Dig into Trump*.

a king who takes care of the world, this metaphor reflects back on humans as kings who have to take care of the world. They have now become lion-like themselves. The rhetorical effect may be clear: humans are depicted as noble, individual, forceful, and male. If humans were metaphorically compared to locusts, this would have another rhetorical effect. They would be a species that appears in masses and devours everything before moving on to the next place. However, if people are compared to locusts, cockroaches, or parasites, this may also have yet another rhetorical effect. It is somehow rendered natural that they are to be destroyed – at least when humans are the so-called caretakers of the world.

We began this chapter with music by father and daughter Ravi and Anoushka Shankar. The piece of music is neither a representation of animals, nor are the tones on which their music is based straightforward references to animals. The music is not a matter of representation, that is. Nevertheless, it is part of a culture that relates to animals rather differently than the average Westerner. For any Westerner who has ever visited India, one of its puzzling elements concerns the way in which Indian people consider cows to be holy.

If the tone 'Re' connotes the bellowing of a mother cow when her calf is taken someplace else, the sound captured in music is not to be taken as a matter of personification. It is rather a matter of mimicry, a term that is defined differently in the humanities and in biology. In the humanities, mimicry was defined, for instance, in the colonial context as a strategy to counter colonial oppression. In mimicking attitudes, clothes, behaviour, or language, colonial subjects could counter a system of othering, but could also inappropriately subvert the colonial distinctions.[12] In biology, scholars distinguish between mimicry as an automatic, or evolutionary process – as when a host of different butterflies show a pattern of eyes on their wings to frighten off predators – and the intentional process of imitating another being.

In our case, we consider mimicry as a subconscious process of imitation, as happens when people yawn, cry, or smile. This is also why yawning has been described as being 'contagious'. Mimicry is not an evolutionary process, in this case, but has a social function that has an intrinsic link with empathy. If people use the term 'imitation' to indicate intentionally replicated behaviour, both mimicry and imitation may be ways through which communication between animals and humans is possible. Some warnings are needed though. Smiling or laughing as a result of which one shows one's teeth is a powerful incentive amongst people to mimic one another, but one should not bare

---

12   On this, see Bhabha, *The Location of Culture.*

one's teeth too easily in front of a chimpanzee, unless one would want to take an explicitly aggressive stance.

In the next part of this chapter we will consider how Frans de Waal, one of the top scholars on primates, defines animal culture on the basis of, firstly, social transmittance and, secondly, novel behaviour that can be transmitted between peers and between generations.[13] We will come to test this definition in relation to our definition of culture and find that De Waal's basic definition entails at least six connections to pivotal elements of ours.

11.2.   Do people have sufficient understanding of animal culture?

WWF-Canada, *Humpback Whale Singing in the Great Bear Sea* (2012)[15]

This part of the chapter discusses whether animals have culture and, by implication, a sense of self. Then we ask whether communication across species is possible. Finally, we will consider whether communication between plants is possible. All these questions have become increasingly urgent due

13   De Waal, *The Ape and the Sushi Master.*
14   For the music, see WWF-Canada, *Humpback Whale Singing in the Great Bear Sea.* For the image, see Herman, *Humpback Whales in Singing Position.*

to a scientific paradigm shift that has been taking place – and that is still taking place. This shift rejects a position according to which animals are considered to be the inferior 'other' of humans, fit for use and exploitation. In contrast, the shift promotes a position that considers humans to be animals that ought to be able to deal with other animals or natural beings on a somewhat equal level. In this context, a term coined by primatologist Frans de Waal is important: 'anthropodenial'.[15] Considering the relations between all sorts of animals and the human animal, De Waal noted that it is pivotal not to deny animals human-like characteristics, such as the use of language, the experience of emotions, or intelligence.

Anthropodenial is clearly at stake when we look at what is being done to animals in bioindustries, or when we consider the destruction of life on this planet. Still, the last few decades have seen a large-scale imagining and re-evaluation of animals in terms of intelligence, emotional sophistication, and social interaction, even though most people will not think of chickens, for instance, as intelligent or emotionally sophisticated beings. This view has been scrutinized, however, as when one scientist aimed to

> examine the peer-reviewed scientific data on the leading edge of cogni-
> tion, emotions, personality, and sociality in chickens, exploring such
> areas as self-awareness, cognitive bias, social learning and self-control,
> and comparing their abilities in these areas with other birds and other
> vertebrates, particularly mammals.[16]

It may be clear that all the terms used when studying animals cannot simply be the same as when they are applied to humans. Rather, the question is whether humans are smart enough to understand the intelligence of other animals.[17]

The necessity to reconsider concepts when comparing animals with the human animal is evident if we consider animals' conception of the individual or the collective self. One of the dominant models to study these phenomena has been self-recognition, which has basically been explored by means of a behaviourist mirror model. Only a small number of species appear to be capable of recognizing themselves in a mirror, like chimpanzees, orang-utans, bonobos, Asian elephants, dolphins, and magpies. Yet why would the human mirror be the only model for assessing whether an animal has a sense of self? We encounter a fundamental problem of translation once

15   De Waal, 'Anthropomorphism and Anthropodenial'.
16   Marino, 'Thinking Chickens'.
17   See a study by De Waal, *Are We Smart Enough*.

again. Animals may well have other forms of individual or collective 'self' when they feel themselves to be located in space and time, in relation to one another and others.

Human assessment of these issues has been hampered by common sense conceptions of brain size and capability. One common hypothesis held that the smaller the brain, the lesser a species' intelligence. The faultiness of such an argument immediately becomes apparent when you consider your current mobile phone to be less powerful than the computers of the 1980s because of its diminutive size. When studying bumble bees, for instance, researchers found that they were very capable of doing rather complicated things. In one study, behavioural ecologist Olli J. Loukola explained that 'in the past, the scientific community has sometimes assumed that the smaller the brain, the less intelligent the species', yet his study proved to be 'the nail in the coffin that that idea is old-fashioned'. His study was in line with 'The Cambridge Declaration on Consciousness', formulated in 2012 at a Cambridge conference where a vast array of scientists from different fields had been re-evaluating the 'conscious experience', and concluded that 'humans are not unique in possessing the neurological substrates that generate consciousness'.[18]

So, however large or small the brain may be, its size does not influence the sense of self. The idea that animals have a sense of self was studied by psychologists Thomas T. Hills and Stephen Butterfill, who examined the ways in which animals forage.[19] They found that animals were not only capable of remembering where they had found resources previously, but were also able to infer where resources could possibly be or how they could get to them by an alternative route, 'akin to realizing that one could go to India by taking a novel route around the earth'.[20] To be able to do this, animals need a primal sense of self, akin to humans saying: 'Suppose I would take this alternative route.'

Most importantly, forms of individual and collective self are at stake when considering the question of whether animals are capable of learning from one another. This issue was at the heart of many studies performed by De Waal who talked about bonding and identification-based observational learning. He was much inspired by the work of Japanese ecologist and anthropologist Kinji Imanishi (1902-1992) who, after studying different groups of macaques, concluded that these groups developed different patterns of behaviour due to

18   Low, 'The Cambridge Declaration on Consciousness', 2.
19   Hills and Butterfill, 'From Foraging to Autonoetic Consciousness'.
20   Ibid., 368.

processes of identification. In fact, Imanishi considered the concept of identification as a fundamental property enjoyed by many, if not all animals. For Imanishi, though, this type of behaviour was precultural because it missed an element of arbitrariness. For instance, in the case of humans, the ways in which they make physical contact in meeting can be radically different, culturally speaking. As was mentioned earlier (cf. Chapter 6), they may hold their hands against one another before their breast, they may lay a hand on their heart, they may shake hands, they may touch elbows, or gently bump fists against one another, and so forth. There is an arbitrary, yet a powerfully symbolic, aspect to this, on the basis of which people recognize one another. Processes of identification and of novel, arbitrary behaviour led De Waal to speak of animal enculturation amongst primates as a matter of intergenerational and peer learning.

One way of comparing humans with animals can be found in cognitive ethology, which studies a generally shared conscious awareness and intention in the behaviour of all animals. Its presupposition is that each animal may live in its own and connected world according to its own capabilities and capacities, but that there are no qualitative differences between animals – only quantitative differences. Culture, in this context, is not specific to humans. In fact, there appear to be more and more species capable of learning by means of identification, imitation, and innovation. The basis of any animal culture then depends on their learning habits that, in the context of already familiar tradition within a given species, can produce a difference.

As we saw in Chapter 3, the political connotes a splitting of worlds, which does not mean that such worlds exist in splendid isolation. Likewise, if each animal lives in its own world, this world is connected to many other worlds in a variety of ways. The fact that all species live in their own world, whether in fauna or flora kinds of surroundings, was defined by scientist Jakob von Uexküll (1864-1944) by way of the term *Umwelt*. Uexküll was among those studying biosemiotics. In this context, he noted that one environment hosts a multiplicity of subjectively defined worlds. Everything that a living entity 'perceives becomes his perceptual world [*Merkwelt*] and all that he does, his effector world [*Wirkwelt*]. Perceptual and effector worlds together form a closed unit, the *Umwelt*.'[21] Translated into current terms, this means that everything an animal is able to perceive (*Merkwelt*) determines its affordances (*Wirkwelt*) and the world in which it lives.

A famous example is the *Umwelt* of ticks. Ticks have their own capacity to (1) smell the odour of Butyric acid, which all mammals emanate; (2) measure temperature, with 37 degrees Celsius being the average temperature of blood

---

21   Uexküll, *A Foray into the Worlds of Animals and Humans*, 6. Originally published in 1934.

mammals; and (3) sense the hairiness of mammals. This makes the tick distinctly different from, say, an octopus. Both live in their distinctive worlds; worlds that are intrinsically connected to others. This is proven by the fact that some octopuses have an incredible capacity to imitate other animals, something a tick could never do, but then again, an octopus is incapable of tracing a slowly moving animal and attaching itself to it without the animal's knowledge.

The connection between any animal's own world and other worlds is a matter of self in the sense of specific capabilities. Ticks, for instance, have what is called Haller's organ, which can be located on the tick's front legs, akin to the human nose. This organ detects odours and chemicals emanating from the host; it senses changes in temperature and air currents; and it can perceive infrared light emanating from a host. Likewise, the fact that cats notice mice, whereas humans often may not, is the result of a cat's capacity to perceive the world in its own specific way. Equally impressive is the fact that some animals are capable of magnetoreception. Scientists have found that 'animals also use the Earth's field lines as magnetic 'signposts' – positional information created by unique combinations of field inclination and intensity at specific geographic locations'.[22] For instance, any pigeon or swift is capable of doing this.

In order to consider the numerous ways in which different worlds connect to one another in terms of relationality, we need to add one pivotal term to the set defined by Uexküll: *Sozialwelt* is a concept 'indicating how individuals of this species usually interact with conspecifics'.[23] Yet in this case we would immediately need to scrutinize the 'social' part in *Sozialwelt*, by expanding it to encompass much more than humanoids capable of communicating with one another. This was argued by Peter Wohlleben in *The Hidden Life of Trees: What They Feel, How They Communicate* (2016). Wohlleben argues that trees of the same species are communal and have evolved in such a way that they can engage in cooperation, and that trees are capable of forming alliances with trees of other species. In terms of intelligence, Wohlleben compares the collective intelligence of trees to that of insect colonies.[24] He is not the sole scholar who contends this, for there is also Stefano Mancuso, with *The Revolutionary Genius of Plants: A New Understanding of Plant Intelligence*, or Suzanne Simard, who empirically proved that plants are able to communicate.[25]

22 Cossins, 'A Sense of Mystery'.
23 Bueno-Guerra, 'How to Apply the Concept of Umwelt'.
24 Wohlleben, *The Hidden Life of Trees*.
25 Simard, *How Trees Talk to Each Other*, 18:10.

The transfer of information over generations of plants and amongst plants was central to the work of Barbara McClintock (1902-1992), who studied something as seemingly simple as maize. Little, however, in this universe is simple. In her case, by closely observing the development of maize for years, she found that genetic information was passed down from one generation of maize to another. For those who think of genes as closed-off boxes, this was an impossibility. Since there was a majority of (male) scientists who thought just this, McClintock at some point stopped publishing about the issue. In a later phase of her career, though, more and more scholars came to see that she had found something that perhaps seemed to be inconceivable, but rather the opposite was true. Likewise, for a long time it seemed inconceivable that humans are the only ones to have moral incentives. Nevertheless, in this case also, primatologists discovered new insights, and the urgent question today is whether only primates have moral consciousness.

We started this chapter with humpback whales 'singing'. What people call singing is a form of communication to whales, or a mixture of singing and talking. Humpback whales have been observed playing with one another and with humans. There have also been moments of conflict with humans, which will not come as a surprise, considering that humans brought them to the verge of extinction.

In the next chapter we will consider in what sense technology can be a matter of culture and ask: how can we study human cultures in relation to media and technologies and how can we conceive of (different) technological cultures? The link between this chapter and the next concerns the *epistemological* question as to what people can know about the conscious lives of animals, or different kinds of robots. The *ontological* issue is whether humans are qualitatively different from either animals or machines, or whether both cases rather suggest a quantitative difference.

12. Culture and Machinic Selves: Artificiality

The Zarathustra Kaaba – Ka'abeye Zartosht
Music: 'Also sprach Zarathustra (2001)' by Deodato (1973)[1]

12.1. Mixtures of being: Have humans always been artificial?

We talked about the issue of nonhuman 'selves' or nonhumans with their own form of self in the previous chapter, and about animals' own cultures as form-of-life. Nevertheless, there are forms of life that do not have culture, or that miss distinct forms of self. Viruses are a good example. They present 'life stripped to the bare essentials. They are the smallest and simplest infectious agents identified to date, [...] little more than a piece of genetic material protected by a protein coat.'[2] Simple as viruses may sound, though,

1 For the music, see Late Night Tales, *Deodato*. For the image, see Javaheri, *Zoroastar Cube*.
2 Crawford, *The Invisible Enemy*, 6.

they can show fascinating effects, as when tulips infected with a certain virus start to show novel varieties in colours; a reason why infected bulbs were cultivated in the seventeenth century to acquire rare varieties of tulips. Yet this is cultivation, not culture.

If we focus on the possibility of technological cultures, their nature coincides only to an extent with the logic and nature of viruses. Viruses are often said to be 'smart', which is an anthropomorphism. They are not smart but they are many: just as one can have powerful computers that are able to handle incredible amounts of data, so can viruses – billions – form a powerful entity. To be able to speak of culture we need a form-of-life and a sense of individual or collective self. Considerable numbers of animals have such forms of culture, and the immediate question is whether technologically construed artefacts can acquire and develop culture. If we assume that culture is both natural and technological in terms of evolution, the development of technology cultures would not be illogical. So, let us first deal with this assumption that culture is both natural and technological.

The first thing to note is that the relation between nature and culture is not one of opposition. Rather, the relation between the two is a matter of subsumption or of distinction, with nature and culture forming the extremes of a scale defined by many differences and varieties. If, in terms of evolution, nature indicates all that exists on this planet, culture is simply one manifestation of what this planet's natural affordances make possible. This is a matter of subsumption. However, if nature includes all living beings and entities on this planet and culture indicates everything that is constructed technically, artificially, this hints at a scale of differences, but again not of opposition. Such an opposition often functions in relation to other, culturally charged oppositions that set up a hierarchy, for instance between civilized and primitive. When nature and culture are not seen as opposites, it becomes possible to see that nature, with its variety of animal cultures, is as much influenced by these cultures, as they are part of, but also co-create natural environments or forms-of-life. Here, the intrinsic correlation between nature and culture has resulted in their conceptual fusion, through the concept of 'natureculture'; a concept introduced by Donna Haraway, an expert in bioscience and technologystudies.[3]

---

3   Donna Haraway, *The Companion Species Manifesto*; also see Hamilton and Neimanis, 'Composting Feminisms'.

When there is no natural or proper state of man, as if humans would be separable from culture, and when culture-as-technique is seen as a natural, evolutionary phenomenon, this implies that humans have persistently been organizing themselves and their world by means of technologies. Such technologies are partly supplementary, but a better way of putting it is that technologies relate to humans in terms of the *prosthetical*. People who miss a leg need a stick or a wheelchair, which becomes an extension of their body.[4] There is an even more fundamental and general prosthetic for the social animals that humans are, namely: language.

One of the explanations as to why humans have evolved so fast is that their major instrument, language, is a form of technology by means of which humans shape one another as sociocultural beings capable of enormous amounts of transfer of knowledge. As philosopher of technology Carl Mitcham explained, the Greek philosopher Plato, via his mouthpiece Socrates, distinguished between two types of *techne*: physical work and speech.[5] The technology of speech is one of the dominant reasons why humans only seemingly coincide with themselves, because they can only coincide with themselves by means of a 'third': language. This dynamic of construction via a third is not neutral and unbiased. Language is at the heart of symbolic orders and, as a consequence, not objective. In this context, the Belgian-French philosopher and linguist Luce Irigaray (1930-) noted that women in European cultures have often been excluded from culture because they have predominantly been given the position of man's so-called natural other. In order for this othering to be dismantled, women need to remake culture. According to Irigaray, they need their own forms of, or other forms of language.

The intrinsic evolutionary relation between humans and technology was central to the work of French philosopher Bernard Stiegler (1952-2020) in a series of volumes entitled *Technics and Time* (1994-2001). The subtitle of part one was telling: 'The fault of Epimetheus'. Epimetheus was the brother of Prometheus. The first name means: 'He who thinks with hindsight', the second one means 'He who thinks ahead'. The Greek gods gave Epimetheus the task of distributing capabilities and characteristics among the animals. However, when he was done distributing, he had nothing left to assign to humans. It had slipped his mind. Humans were to live as faulty animals, then. As a compromise, Prometheus endowed them with the civilizing arts – he

---

4   For an example of this, see Polak, *FDR in American Memory*.
5   Mitcham, 'Philosophy and the History of Technology', 173.

stole fire from the gods to provide humans with this powerful technology. The story illustrates that humans are adoptive creatures, whose lives are made possible by 'prosthetic' tools.

There is a constitutive correlation, then, between the human subject (the 'who') and the technical object (the 'what'). Consequently, it is only possible to think of humans as intrinsically *impure*, or as a *mixture*, which happens to be the original meaning of 'corrupt'. With respect to this, as already indicated, it is beside the point to consider humans as merely using technology. Rather, they live in symbiosis with it. As in-betweens of animal-like and artificial beings, humans are mixtures, who over the last centuries actively developed yet other mixtures of being and beings. Stanley Kubrick's movie 2001: A SPACE ODYSSEY (1968) is one palpable example thereof. In this movie a computer-being called HAL 9000 is capable of overruling the human astronauts, if necessary, for the survival of the ship and its mission, or for HAL's mission. The name HAL is derived from '*H*euristically programmed *AL*gorithmic computer'. Since 1968, computers and robotic entities came to be increasingly associated with algorithms.

Culturally speaking, it is of interest to note that the term 'algorithm' is derived from an eighth-century Persian astronomer and mathematician called Muḥammad ibn Mūsā al-Khwārizmī, whose last name was Latinized as Algo-rithmi. Algorithms are systematically calculable. Within a computer context they indicate a sequence of systematically related rule-bound instructions that can solve something on the basis of automized 'reasoning'. If one famous example is how to find the largest number in a set of randomly organized numbers, then it is easy to imagine how algorithms can be used to work in relation to humans. Suppose one considers Facebook as a set of randomly ordered data. One can use algorithms to find out, then, which person or persons will be inclined to do or think X. It just requires a sequence of systematically related rule-bound instructions and computers that can deal with masses of information. Suppose these algorithms find who is fond of wild gardening and who isn't. Then, a second set can be employed concerning the question: if people like wild gardening, what is the political party they will be inclined to vote for? Or: what is their favorite type of holidays? Or: what are their favorite pets? Or: what kinds of diseases do they tend to have? If the answers to all such questions are combined, this leads to profiles that provide valuable information for political parties, industries, insurance companies, and so forth.

Instead of considering this only as a threatening trend, Haraway saw it as a development that forces us to rethink the nature of humans and the ways in which they organize their worlds in terms of power. Her essay 'A Cyborg Manifesto: Science, Technology, and Socialist-Feminism in the Late Twentieth

Century' was first published in 1985 and then as part of a book in 1991.[6] Haraway traces three 'boundary breakdowns' since the twentieth century. It concerns the boundaries between human and animal, between animal-human and machine, and between the physical and the non-physical. These boundaries have been crossed due to a specific technological development:

> Writing, power, and technology are old partners in Western stories of the origin of civilization, but miniaturization has changed our experience of mechanism. Miniaturization has turned out to be about power; small is not so much beautiful as pre-eminently dangerous, as in cruise missiles.[7]

Due to miniaturizations of technology, so Haraway states, a new being has become possible, which she called a *cyborg*, an acronym for *cyb*ernetic *org*anism. This is an artificial being that can develop itself by learning – one of the pivotal aspects of culture. The term 'cybernetics' was coined in 1948 by mathematician Norbert Wiener, in *Cybernetics, or Control and Communication in the Animal and the Machine*. Wiener was discussing certain feedback loops that are similar in animals and machines. Twentieth-century machinic technologies blurred the lines between natural and artificial, for example, when robots assembled cars as accurately as humans, or once robots could move like animals. Moreover, microelectronics and the political invisibility of cyborgs came to blur notions of physicality and non-physicality. For instance, vast computers currently control most of the flows of investments and money across the globe without any specific human actor pulling the strings – or being responsible.

The accelerating process of human technologies has altered human subjectivity, changed modes of cultural interaction, and has led to shifting epistemological and ontological distinctions. With epistemology the key issue is what people can know. The Turing test is an epistemological test in that it tries to find out whether some entity is a human or a computer. Yet once this is established, it leads to ontological decisions in the sense that the two are then ontologically placed under one category or the other, and these categories come with their own characteristics. Humans are 'natural', for instance, and computers are 'artificial'.

Now that human environments and human bodies themselves have become increasingly artificial, the question arises how humans can still be defined as somehow 'natural'. The latter notion remains attractive because it connotes origins, primacies, and fundaments. Since the beginning of the nineteenth

---

6   Haraway, *Simians, Cyborgs and Women*.
7   Ibid., 153.

century, one tactic has been to set up the human self against an 'other' – in this case an artificial one. This was, on the one hand, a familiar colonial tactic (cf. Chapter 8). On the other hand, the artificial other functioned as a counterpart which had the effect that humans were considered 'natural'. In the colonial case, an opposition was set up between civilized people and those who still lived backwardly, in nature. In the technological case, the scales were reversed: so-called natural humans were placed in opposition to artificial entities.

One of the first famous novels in which this was worked out is Mary Shelley's *Frankenstein, or The Modern Prometheus* (1818, with a reworked edition from 1831). The novel shows how a humanoid creature is made by chemically producing and gluing together different body parts. Once it has come alive, it starts to wonder what it is:

> And what was I? Of my creation and creator I was absolutely ignorant; but I knew that I possessed no money, no friends, no kind of property. I was, besides, endued with a figure hideously deformed and loathsome; I was not even of the same nature as man. I was more agile than they, and could subsist upon coarser diet; I bore the extremes of heat and cold with less injury to my frame; my stature far exceeded theirs. When I looked around, I saw and heard of none like me. Was I then a monster, a blot upon the earth, from which all men fled, and whom all men disowned?[8]

Frankenstein is only the first of many creatures and numerous similar characters followed, such as Roy from the movie BLADE RUNNER (1982). Artificial beings are the mirror image of humans in all these cases, and in many instances they are stronger, or (more) monstrous. Still, as such they are also the embodiment of, or the reflection of the principally alienated status of humans themselves. We dealt with this alienated status earlier, when considering Slavoj Žižek's response to BLADE RUNNER (cf. Chapter 7). The colonial dynamic scrutinized was that some define themselves in relation to an ideologically constructed other. With technology, humans' artificial others are literally made by humans, and then start to have a life of their own. This does not concern an opposition between two worlds, but rather a multiplication of worlds.

This part of the chapter started with a piece of music by Brazilian composer and musician Eumir Deodato, entitled 'Also sprach Zarathustra (2001)'. It was released in 1973 as a jazzy reworking of a composition by classical German composer Richard Strauss from 1896, 'Also sprach Zarathustra'. This, in turn,

8   Shelley, *Frankenstein*, 103.

was a symphonic response to Friedrich Nietzsche's philosophical fiction with the same title written in the 1880s. In his last work, Nietzsche used the old Persian or Iranian prophet as a mouthpiece for what he thought himself. Zarathustra, according to the latest assessments, lived between 1400 and 1200 BCE, in another world. Nietzsche, living more than three thousand years later, is distinctly modern. As such, he was well aware of the latest evolutionary insights. In this context, he described modern humans as a phase in-between the phase of primates and the phase of 'superseded' man; or what Nietzsche called *Übermensch*. If this new kind of human being was capable of embracing its fate (*amor fati*), it would be able to create radically new values through novel creations. Nietzsche was rather optimistic about these new creations. However, his concept of the *Übermensch* was highjacked by the Nazis, and consequently lost much of its indication that there might come an evolutionary phase after this one in which the human will be superseded.

We will focus on the consequences of new technological possibilities in the next part, by distinguishing between (1) the technologization of culture; (2) the culturalization of technologies; and (3) technological cultures. The latter concerns the possible succession of human order as we know it – or knew it.

12.2.   What are the multiple relations between culture and technology?

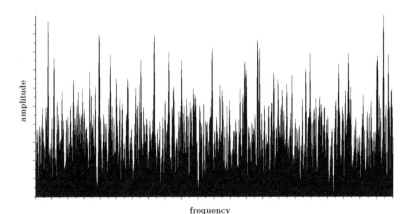

Visualization of White Noise[9]
Music: György Ligeti, 'Atmosphères' (1961)[10]

9   Debianux, *Spectrogram of a White Noise.*
10   France Musique, *Ligeti: Atmosphères.*

We started this book with the question of why culture is a matter of life and death. To be sure, throughout history different powers have dealt with life and death, using different technologies to distribute both. In certain cultures, it was acceptable to kill baby girls, for instance, in others it was accepted to kill handicapped children, and in some cultures human sacrifice was central. However, from the eighteenth century onwards, societies have been organized by means of what has been defined as *biopower*, the power to decide over societal forms of life and death, or *biopolitics* as Foucault and in his wake Antonio Negri defined it: the calculated, politico-economical organization of life and death. This biopower or biopolitics is different from what has come to be known as *biotechnology* since the 1950s.

Capitalism and technology have enjoyed a happy symbiosis from the start. The issue of this symbiosis in the present is whether, due to miniaturization and acceleration, new and more autonomous technologies are developing. If so, this implies a change in the nature of politics and the political, a change in human subjectivity, and a change in the scope of what culture used to indicate. The political change was already sensed by Hannah Arendt in *The Human Condition* from 1958, in which she argued that the capacity to actively construct the world, or the world anew, has become a matter of technologies rather than politics.

In order to assess what is new, here, we need to distinguish between three different forms of the relation between technology and culture:

(1) When we speak of the *technologization of culture*, we are referring to the ways in which forms of technology have influenced both culture with a small 'c' and with a capital 'C'. The advent of paper, for instance, not only facilitated new ways of communication or the spread and preservation of knowledge, but also made new forms of art possible. As a consequence, a paper-culture was distinctly different from cultures that did not have paper. The same applies to the invention of the printing press. In both cases new media were pivotal – and note that 'media' is used as a plural of *medium* here; the use of media in the singular is specific for 'new media'. Other devices or instruments would have equally great impacts. The astrolabe helped sailors in the Mediterranean, in the Middle East, and along the African and Indian coasts to identify their exact position at sea. The pendulum clock helped propel the colonial endeavours in the seventeenth century, because it was the first clock that also functioned on ships. All technological events and media introduced new themes in art and literature, new art forms, but also new experiences, new affects, or new diseases. All these processes could also provoke new genres, as when the late nineteenth century witnessed

the appearance of the genre of science fiction that presented future states of affairs and scenarios – though mostly as a reflection of what was already the case or almost the case.

(2) A second relation between technology and culture can be entitled the *culturalization of technology*. In this case it concerns the ways in which the same kind of technology operates differently in the context of different cultures. The principle of a windmill is the same everywhere, for instance, yet the ways in which windmills were built and used in Spain is rather different from the ways in which they have been set up in the Netherlands. In Spain, windmills were never used for dry-milling lakes, whereas the Netherlands made this its primary focus for some time. Different species of horses used to live in the Americas, up until between 13,000 and 7500 years ago, when they became extinct. Horses were brought back to the Americas by the Spanish and were rapidly adopted by Native Americans, who used them in a different way than the Spanish or English did. The new situation came to be felt as 'natural' so quickly that some Native American nations started being called 'the people of the horse'. Or, to give another example, gunpowder had a universally similar mixture of chemicals, but was used in different ways. At some point in China, during a period that was mostly peaceful, it was used as a matter of fun, for fireworks. The Mongols started to use it as a weapon by making flying fire. Middle Eastern or European powers started to use it for canons in the fourteenth century.

(3) With the arrival of *technological cultures* we are describing cultures of technologies themselves: technological entities that are capable of learning and transmitting knowledge to peers and further generations of technological entities. This possibility was developed by French philosopher Gilbert Simondon (1924-1989) when he considered evolutionary machines to be open entities rather than closed ones. He pitched this idea when working towards a general phenomenology of machines and his prediction was that machines will have an evolution of their own.[11] In this context, he argued against the idea of cybernetics as the sole determiner of machines. According to Simondon, cybernetics accepted 'what every theory of technology must refuse: a classification of technological objects according to pre-established criteria and following genera and species'.[12] Rather, Simondon wanted to consider individuated machines that functioned in their own right

11   Simondon, 'The Essence of Technicity' and 'The Limits of Human Progress'.
12   Simondon, *Du mode d'existence des objets techniques*, 48.

and capacity in what Uexküll had defined as *Umwelt*. Another argument was proposed by the already mentioned Donna Haraway, who in 'Cyborg Manifesto', envisioned that boundaries between human beings and others would become more fluid and that new forms of subjectivity would come to exist. Although Haraway focused more on 'natureculture' her ideas imply that different technological naturecultures can come to exist.

The issue of whether artificial entities are capable of, or allowed to function in their own right and capacity has become a vexing one. Media scholar Alexander Galloway considered this new phenomenon in a study entitled *Protocol: How Control Exists after Decentralization* in which he argued against the idea of the internet being a free space, but rather one dominated by asymmetries. More importantly in the context of our argument, Galloway emphasized the fact that computers work on the basis of different codes, which in turn imply different forms of organization and culture.[13] Now, the current situation may suggest that it is still humans who are doing the controlling and codifying. Nevertheless, as soon as computers or computer systems acquire their own capacities with respect to this, this forces us to rethink the very idea of anthropocentrism. Whereas some humans, whether helped by fictional divine forces or not, used to consider themselves to be the sovereigns of the planet, they have now come to produce entities that may transcend this notion of supremacy.

The implications can be sensed with regard to all levels of life. To take just one: will the issue of justice remain the same in situations that artificial intelligence equals or transcends that of humans? If laws would move from unquestionable human *sovereignty* to equality before a newly defined law or a newly conceived judge, this may sound abstract but becomes less so once we consider it in terms of cultural interactions that exceed the limits of human cultures.[14] There is a considerable number of literary works and movies by now that sketch alternate realities in which different forms of robots or computers connote different forms of artificial intelligence, and of culture. In many instances, these new forms do not just communicate with humans, but also judge them, or correct them, or punish them.

In a context in which humans come to live with artificial beings that are equally smart, or smarter, or smart in another way, we might have to critically reassess a dominant Christian narrative that frames the first

---

13   Galloway, *Protocol*.
14   On this possibility, see Korsten and De Zeeuw, 'Towards a New Judicial Scene for Humans and Animals'.

artificial beings by divine sovereignty. This is how it is told in the biblical book *Genesis* 2:

> [18] Then the Lord God said, 'It is not good that the man should be alone; I will make him a helper fit for him.' [19] Now out of the ground the Lord God had formed every beast of the field and every bird of the heavens and brought them to the man to see what he would call them. And whatever the man called every living creature, that was its name. [20] The man gave names to all livestock and to the birds of the heavens and to every beast of the field. But for Adam there was not found a helper fit for him. [21] So the Lord God caused a deep sleep to fall upon the man, and while he slept took one of his ribs and closed up its place with flesh. [22] And the rib that the Lord God had taken from the man he made into a woman and brought her to the man. [23] Then the man said,
> 'This at last is bone of my bones
> and flesh of my flesh;
> she shall be called Woman,
> because she was taken out of Man.'
> [24] Therefore a man shall leave his father and his mother and hold fast to his wife, and they shall become one flesh. [25] And the man and his wife were both naked and were not ashamed.[15]

The biblical story has been incredibly influential. If we take it at face value, God acts in it as a magician who uses language to make life. He is a technician or an engineer who builds a garden according to a plan. He is a bioengineer who makes another human from the material of an already existing one. And he is a ruler, for he creates a hierarchy of powers in the world now that the original human is split into a man and a woman, with the latter being a derivative of the former. As a result, and despite the divine intervention, the world becomes *anthropomorphic*. Life is split up into *zoë* (all living matter) and *bios* (organized life).

The current difficulty is whether we can extend the notion of life to technological beings. If this happens, it entails, as said, vast implications for the very idea of human political and legal supremacy, it involves novel problems of hegemony, of understanding, of translation, and of cultural interactions.

The music that opened this part of the chapter – György Ligeti's 'Atmosphères' – may illustrate what possible problems of communication could be.

15   Gen 2:18-24 ESV.

First of all, there is the element of harmony, an element often associated with music. This is not a universal given. Different cultures work with different forms of harmony (cf. Chapter 11). Defining music as harmonious or not is yet again different from the issue of what counts as 'noise'. Ligeti liked to work with noise, also technological noise, like *sine waves*, or so-called 'white noise', forms of sounds that he called 'artificial phonemes'. Moreover, he liked to work with the technological capacities to mix and remix.[16] Ligeti organized noise in a certain way then, to make music. This is why critic Alex Ross could say that Ligeti was making 'otherworldly music' and was 'searching for music's outer limits'.[17]

As for 'other-worldly music', many movies involving extraterrestrials use music, or an organization of sound, to demonstrate possible communication. For instance, in Stephen Spielberg's movie CLOSE ENCOUNTERS OF THE THIRD KIND (1977), humans and the extraterrestrials come to commune by means of some sort of harmonious music. It made one viewer remark, 'Thank God the extraterrestrials do not like heavy metal.' In the case of ARRIVAL (2016), a movie by Denis Villeneuve, the problem of cultural interaction and translation is a central theme, featuring extraterrestrials that are heptapods and look like giant octopuses. Their sounds and language, or their culture, is not marked by linearity. As a result, the main protagonist, a language expert, has to discover how radically other forms of language are translatable. Meanwhile, the heptapods sound like whales or elephants in the film. With respect to this, it is telling that elephants may communicate with one another at levels so low that humans cannot hear them.

One question here is, if technological cultures are to develop, whether such cultures consider humans to be an important species to communicate and interact with. Perhaps they would rather opt to communicate with one another. One other question is whether humans will be smart enough to perceive any such communication. Imagine, for instance, forms of intelligence that have culture, but communicate by means beyond the outer limits of what humans can perceive. Or humans would only perceive this as noise, not as expression, or meaningful communication. The problem is both similar to and different from sounds that are too low or too high to be heard. Technology may help humans, here, but there is always a limit, as we already discovered when dealing with the issue of translation (cf. Chapter 9).

It is a recurring fantasy of humans, expressed in a host of literary texts, comics, and movies, that they will be able to communicate, cross-culturally,

---

16 A standard work on this type of music is Holmes, *Electronic and Experimental Music*.
17 Ross, 'Ligeti 1993'.

and interculturally with other forms of intelligent beings. Nonetheless, such other beings may be able to communicate, or express themselves, beyond what humans are able to perceive. Or, they may not even notice humans. This does not mean that conflict will be the inevitable result, or that cooperation is impossible. However, such cooperation will inevitably be one-sided, just as when humans, for instance, use worms to make compost. And who or what would listen to worms? Or, to rephrase this rhetorical question: suppose some extremely advanced form of intelligence considered humans to be somehow on the scale of worms. Then humans would probably object to their not being heard. The fictive example can help to make music out of what only seems to be noise. What a different world it would be, in terms of conflict and cooperation, if people were willing and capable of listening to worms, instead of only using them for cultivation, or drowning them by means of excessive fertilization.

Postscript: On a Note of Justice

Some decades ago, a legal case was brought to the International Court of Justice in The Hague that appeared to be about the construction of a couple of dams on the Danube. It concerned the Gabčíkovo-Nagymaros Project that involved the states of Czechoslovakia and Hungary, and after 1993 that of the Czech Republic, Slovakia, and Hungary. It appeared that major ecological issues had not been involved in the decision-making process which led to the construction of the dams. Hungary, in this case, was reluctant to work together on the project any longer because ecological issues had become a matter of concern.

Now, Hungary's refusal to go along in the construction of the dams threatened to lead to a conflict, which is why the case was brought to the International Court of Justice (cf. Chapter 2). The court came to a decision in 1997. To defend his decision in the case, one of the judges, Christopher Weeramantry (1926-2017), used Article 9 of the Statute of the International Court of Justice.[1] This article requires the 'representation of the *main forms of civilization* and of the principal legal systems of the world' (emphasis added by the judge).[2] The mentioned 'main forms of civilization' were not just existing ones, however, but also previous ones. Weeramantry's argument was that ecological issues demand a wisdom that goes beyond the interests of the present.

Weeramantry's argument was included in a compilation on international law on the protection of the environment which held that ecological issues should answer 'not only to principles common to the major legal families today, but also to certain fundamental ideas embraced by all the cultures and civilisations throughout history'.[3] Apparently, the issue was – and is – that conflict can be solved by cooperation, if humans are smart enough to expand the limits of their intercultural communication and understanding across time, across cultures, across species and as we have seen – perhaps – across machinic beings.

---

1 On Judge Weeramantry's motivation, see International Court of Justice, 'Separate Opinion'.
2 For the article, see International Court of Justice, 'Statute of the International Court of Justice'.
3 Bowman, Davies and Redgwell, *Lyster's International Wildlife Law*, 34.

Bibliography

Abebe, Alpha. 'Afropolitanism: Global Citizenship with African Routes'. *OxPol* (blog), 10 April 2015. https://blog.politics.ox.ac.uk/afropolitanism-global-citizenship-with-african-routes/.

Adair-Toteff, Christopher. 'Ferdinand Tönnies: Utopian Visionary'. *Sociological Theory* 13, no. 1 (1995): 58-65.

Agamben, Giorgio. *Means without End: Notes on Politics.* Translated by Vincenzo Binetti and Cesare Casarino. Minneapolis: University of Minnesota Press, 2000.

Alchetron. 'Art Spiegelman'. 30 May 2018. http://alchetron.com/Art-Spiegelman-435777-W.

Andrews, Julie. 'The Sound of Music'. By Oscar Hammerstein II and Richard Rodgers. First released on 2 March 1965. Track 1 on *The Sound of Music.* Soundtrack, Mercury Records, 1965, CD.

Aristotle, Portland. 'The Rise of China Refutes "End of History" Theory, Francis Fukuyama Admits to a Shocked Powell's Books Audience'. *The Oregonian,* 14 April 2011. https://www.oregonlive.com/myoregon/2011/04/the_rise_of_china_refutes_end.html.

Assouline, Pierre. *Hergé: The Man Who Created Tintin.* Translated by Charles Ruas. Oxford: Oxford University Press, 2011.

Barthes, Ronald. 'Toward a Psychosociology of Contemporary Food Consumption'. In *Food and Culture: A Reader,* 3rd ed., edited by Carole Counihan and Penny Van Esterik, 23-30. New York: Routledge, 2013.

Basson, Adriaan. 'The Dream Truths of Notrose Konile'. *Mail & Guardian,* 5 June 2009. https://mg.co.za/article/2009-06-05-the-dream-truths-of-notrose-konile/.

Bauman, Zygmunt. 'Making and Unmaking of Strangers'. *Thesis Eleven* 43, no. 1 (1995): 1-16.

Beethoven, Ludwig van. *Symphonie nr 9, Partiturerstausgabe.* Mainz: Schott, o. J, [1926]. Wikimedia Commons, illustration. https://commons.wikimedia.org/wiki/File:Beethoven_-_Symphonie_Nr.9,_Partiturerstausgabe_1826.pdf.

Best, Shaun. *The Stranger.* London: Routledge, 2019.

Bhabha, Homi K.. *The Location of Culture.* London: Routledge, 1994.

Bhatt, Chetan. *Hindu Nationalism: Origins, Ideologies and Modern Myths.* New York: Berg, 2001.

Block, Pamela, Devva Kasnitz, Akemi Nishida and Nick Pollard, eds. *Occupying Disability: Critical Approaches to Community, Justice, and Decolonizing Disability.* Dordrecht: Springer, 2016.

Boonzaier, Floretta, and Taryn van Niekerk. *Decolonial Feminist Community Psychology.* New York: Springer, 2019.

Bowman, Michael, Peter Davies and Catherine Redgwell, eds., *Lyster's International Wildlife Law*. Cambridge: Cambridge University Press, 2010.

Brooks, Daphne A. '"This Voice Which Is Not One": Amy Winehouse Sings the Ballad of Sonic Blue(s)face Culture'. *Women & Performance: A Journal of Feminist Theory* 20, no. 1 (2010): 37-60. https://doi.org/10.1080/07407701003589337.

Brown, Wendy. *Regulating Aversion: Tolerance in the Age of Identity and Empire*. Princeton, NJ: Princeton University Press, 2006.

Bueno-Guerra, Nereida. 'How to Apply the Concept of Umwelt in the Evolutionary Study of Cognition'. *Frontiers in Psychology* 9 (2018): 1-3. https://doi.org/10.3389/fpsyg.2018.02001.

Burke, Peter. *What Is Cultural History?* Hoboken: Wiley, 2019.

Butler, Judith. *Gender Trouble: Feminism and the Subversion of Identity*. New York: Routledge, 2006.

Canetti, Elias. *Crowds and Power*. Translated by Carol Stewart. New York: The Viking Press, 1962.

Carters, The. 'Apeshit'. First released on 16 June 2018. Track 2 on *Everything Is Love*. Parkwood Entertainment, Sony Music Entertainment, Roc Nation, 2018.

Catenaccio, Claire. 'Oedipus Tyrannus: The Riddle of the Feet'. *The Classical Outlook* 89, no. 4 (2012): 102-107.

CBS. 'Studenten lenen vaker en meer'. October 2019. https://www.cbs.nl/nl-nl/nieuws/2019/41/studentenlenen-vaker-en-meer.

Centurion0192. *Lucille Bogan – B.D. Woman's Blues (1935)*. YouTube, 9 November 2011, video, 2:58. https://www.youtube.com/watch?v=_nmrWB1ovQo.

CNN. *Watch Obama Dig into Trump at the 2011 White House Corres....* YouTube, 29 April 2016, video, 5:09. https://www.youtube.com/watch?v=HHckZCxdRkA.

Coaston, Jane. 'The Intersectionality Wars'. *Vox*, 28 May 2019. https://www.vox.com/the-highlight/2019/5/20/18542843/intersectionality-conservatism-law-race-gender-discrimination.

Cossins, Dan. 'A Sense of Mystery'. *The Scientist*, 1 August 2013. https://www.the-scientist.com/coverstory/a-sense-of-mystery-38949.

Cover, Robert. 'Nomos and Narrative'. In *Narrative, Violence, and the Law: The Essays of Robert* Cover, edited by Martha Minow, Michael Ryan and Austin Sarat, 95-172. Ann Arbor: The University of Michigan Press, 1995.

Crawford, Dorothy H. *The Invisible Enemy: A Natural History of Viruses*. Oxford: Oxford University Press, 2000.

Crenshaw, Kimberlé. 'Demarginalizing the Intersection of Race and Sex: A Feminist Critique of Antidiscrimination Doctrine, Feminist Theory and Antiracist Politics'. *University of Chicago Legal Forum* 1989, no. 1 (1989): 139-167. http://chicagounbound.uchicago.edu/uclf/vol1989/iss1/8.

Crenshaw, Kimberlé, and Abby Dobson. *The Urgency of Intersectionality*. TED, 15 October 2016, video, 18:40. https://www.ted.com/talks/kimberle_crenshaw_the_urgency_of_intersectionality?referrer=playlist-10_great_talks_to_celebrate_bl.

Crocq, Marc-Antoine. 'Historical and Cultural Aspects of Man's Relationships with Addictive Drugs'. *Dialogues in Clinical Neuroscience* 9, no. 4 (2007): 355-361.

Cryle, Peter, and Elizabeth Stephens. *Normality: A Critical Genealogy*. Chicago: University of Chicago Press, 2017.

Dalbéra, Jean-Pierre. *Lélue (Sacre du printemps, ballets russes)*. Wikimedia Commons, 26 April 2010, image. https://commons.wikimedia.org/wiki/File:Lélue_(Sacre_du_printemps,_ballets_russes)_(4557057918).jpg.

Davis, Angela Y. *Women, Culture & Politics*. New York: Random House, 1989.

Davis-Floyd, Robbie E., and Carolyn F. Sargent. *Childbirth and Authoritative Knowledge: Cross-Cultural Perspectives*. Berkeley: University of California Press, 1997.

Debianux. *Spectrogram of a White Noise*. Wikimedia Commons, 25 September 2008, image. https://commons.wikimedia.org/wiki/File:Spectrogram_white_noise.png.

Deleuze, Gilles. 'Postscript on the Societies of Control'. *October 59* (1992): 3-7.

De Waal, Frans. 'Anthropomorphism and Anthropodenial: Consistency in Our Thinking about Humans and Other Animals'. *Zoological Philosophy* 27, no. 1 (1999): 255-280.

—. *The Ape and the Sushi Master: Cultural Reflections by a Primatologist*. New York: Basic Books, 2001.

—. *Are We Smart Enough to Know How Smart Animals Are?* New York: Norton, 2016.

De Zeeuw, Tessa. 'Encountering the Law: Machinic and Theatrical Space in Criminal Prosecution'. In *Legibility in the Age of Signs and Machines*, edited by Pepita Hesselberth, Janna Houwen, Esther Peeren and Ruby de Vos, 113-130. https://doi.org/10.1163/9789004376175_009.

Dirks, Nicholas B. *Castes of Mind: Colonialism and the Making of Modern India*. Princeton, NJ: Princeton University Press, 2001.

Durkheim, Émile. *The Elementary Forms of Religious Life*. Translated by Carol Cosman. Oxford: Oxford University Press, 2008.

Durkheim, E., and M. Mauss. 'Note on the Notion of Civilization'. In *Classical Readings in Culture and Civilization*, edited by John Rundell and Stephen Mennell, 151-154. London: Routledge, 1998.

Dury, Ian. 'Spasticus Autisticus'. First released in 1981. Track 8 on *Lord Upminster*. Polydor Records Ltd., 1981, CD.

Dussel, Enrique. *Ethics of Liberation in the Age of Globalization and Exclusion*. Translated by E. Mendieta, C. P. Bustillo, Y. Angulo and N. Maldonado-Torres. Durham, NC: Duke University Press, 2013.

—. *Twenty Theses on Politics*. Translated by George Ciccariello-Maher. Durham, NC: Duke University Press, 2008.

Dylan, Bob. 'Man Gave Names to All the Animals'. Track 8 on *Slow Train Coming*, Columbia Records, 1979, CD.

Eagle Rock Café. 'How to Taste Coffee and Become a Coffee Aficionado'. Eagle Rock Café website, 28 June 2019. https://eaglerockcafe.com/how-to-taste-coffee-become-a-coffee-aficionado/

Easterling, Keller. *Extrastatecraft: The Power of Infrastructure Space*. London: Verso, 2014.

El2546. *Ravi & Anoushka Shankar*. YouTube, 24 November 2018, video, 53:56. https://www.youtube.com/watch?v=lIQrUZLyAT0.

Engelenhoven, Gerlov van. '"Whereof One Cannot Speak…": Deceptive Voices and Agentive Silences in the Articulation of Identities of the Moluccan Postcolonial Migrant Community in the Netherlands. PhD diss., University of Giessen, 2020.

Esposito, Roberto. *Communitas: The Origin and Destiny of Community*. Translated by Timothy Campbell. Stanford: Stanford University Press, 2009.

Fernández, Raquel. 'Culture and Economics'. In *The New Palgrave Dictionary of Economics*, 1-10. London: Palgrave Macmillan UK, 2016. https://doi.org/10.1057/978-1-349-95121-5_2192-1.

Flanigan, James. 'Pinochet Aside, Chile's Reforms Launched a New Era'. *Los Angeles Times*, 15 March 1998. https://www.latimes.com/archives/la-xpm-1998-mar-15-fi-29059-story.html.

Foucault, Michel. *Power/Knowledge: Selected Interviews and Other Writings 1972-1977*. London: Random House, 1980.

France Musique. *Ligeti: Atmosphères*. YouTube, 25 March 2019, video, 9:06. https://www.youtube.com/watch?v=jUaPwTL5vL8.

Franklin, Aretha. 'Amazing Grace'. By John Newton and William Walker. First released on 1 June 1972. Track 12 on *Amazing Grace: The Complete Recordings*. Atlantic Recording Corporation, 1972, CD.

Freud, Sigmund. *Civilization and Its Discontents*. Translated by James Strachey. New York: W. W. Norton, 1962.

—. *Das Unbehagen in der Kultur*. Wien: Internationaler Psychoanalytischer Verlag, 1930.

Fukuyama, Francis. 'The End of History?' *The National Interest* 16 (Summer 1989).

Galloway, Alexander. *Protocol: How Control Exists after Decentralization*. Cambridge, MA: MIT Press, 2004.

Gao, Ricky. 'The Sustainability of Salmon Farming in BC'. Just Another UBC Blogs Site (blog). 14 October 2015. https://blogs.ubc.ca/rickygao/.

Geertz, Clifford. *The Interpretation of Cultures*. New York: Basic Books, 1973.

Geffen, Sasha. 'How Pop Music Broke the Gender Binary'. *The Paris Review* (blog), 16 April 2020. https://www.theparisreview.org/blog/2020/04/16/how-pop-music-broke-the-gender-binary/.

—. 'Synthesizing Sound and Self: The Vexed Legacy of Electronic Music Pioneer Wendy Carlos'. *The Nation*, 15 October 2020. https://www.thenation.com/article/culture/wendy-carlos-biography-review/.

Gibson, James Jerome. *The Ecological Approach to Visual Perception*. Boston/London: Houghton Mifflin, 1979.

Gibson-Graham, J.K. 'Diverse Economies: Performative Practices for "Other Worlds"'. *Progress in Human Geography*, 32, no. 5 (2008). https://doi.org/10.1177/0309132508090821.

Glissant, Edouard. *Poetics of Relation*. Translated by Betsy Wing. Ann Arbor: University of Michigan Press, 1997.

Gomez, Carlos. 'Giving Birth Upright, with Maté – Peru Clinics Open Arms to Indigenous Women'. United Nations Population Fund, 29 September 2016. https://www.unfpa.org/news/giving-birth-upright-maté---peru-clinics-open-arms-indigenous-women.

Grck7. *The Right to Live in Peace – Chilean Artists. English Subtitles. Victor Jara – El derecho de vivir en paz*. YouTube, 8 November 2019, video, 3:47. https://www.youtube.com/watch?v=bI3GlSkZmyo.

Graeber, David. *Debt: The First 5,000 Years*. Brooklyn, NY: Melville House, 2011.

—. *Toward an Anthropological Theory of Value: The False Coin of Our Own Dreams*. New York: Palgrave Macmillan, 2001.

Großbölting, Thomas. *Losing Heaven: Religion in Germany since 1945*. Translated by Alex Skinner. New York: Berghahn Books, 2017.

Gwet, Yann. 'Pour la France, le vrai "défi civilisationnel" envers l'Afrique est simple: ne plus rien faire!' *Le Monde*, 12 July 2017. https://www.lemonde.fr/afrique/article/2017/07/12/pour-la-france-le-vrai-deficivilisationnel-envers-l-afrique-est-simple-ne-plus-rien-faire_5159511_3212.html.

Hahn, Harlan. 'The Political Implications of Disability Definitions and Data'. *Journal of Disability Policy Studies* 4, no. 2 (1993): 41-52. https://doi.org/10.1177/104420739300400203.

Hamilton, Jennifer Mae, and Astrida Neimanis. 'Composting Feminisms and Environmental Humanities'. *Environmental Humanities* 10, no. 2 (2018): 501-527.

Hannerz, Ulf. *Cultural Complexity: Studies in the Social Organization of Meaning*. New York: Columbia University Press, 1992.

Haraway, Donna. 'A Cyborg Manifesto: Science, Technology, and Socialist-Feminism in the Late Twentieth Century'. In *Simians, Cyborgs and Women: The Reinvention of Nature* New York; Routledge, 1991; 149-181.

——. *The Companion Species Manifesto: Dogs, People, and Significant Otherness*. Chicago: Prickly Paradigm Press, 2003.

Harrison, George. 'Bangla Desh'. First release on 28 September 1971. Track 4 on *The Concert for Bangladesh*. Apple Records, 1971.

Hellemans, Babette. *Understanding Culture: A Handbook for Students in the Humanities*. Amsterdam: Amsterdam University Press, 2017.

Herman, Louis M. *Humpback Whales in Singing Position*. Wikimedia Commons, March 2005 or earlier, photograph. https://commons.wikimedia.org/wiki/File:Humpback_whales_in_singing_position.jpg.

Hills, Thomas T., and Stephen Butterfill. 'From Foraging to Autonoetic Consciousness: The Primal Self as a Consequence of Embodied Prospective Foraging'. *Current Zoology* 61, no. 2 (2015): 368-381. https://doi.org/10.1093/czoolo/61.2.368.

Hirst, Paul. 'Endism: Why 1989 Was Not the "End of History"'. *Open Democracy*, 20 November 2019. https://www.opendemocracy.net/en/endism/.

Hiskes, Andries. 'Drawn to Deviance: The Deformed Body Exhibited'. Leidenartsinsocietyblog, 21 November 2019. https://www.leidenartsinsocietyblog.nl/articles/drawn-to-deviance-the-deformed-body-exhibited.

Hofstede, Geert, and Gert Jan Hofstede. 'Geert Hofstede and Gert Jan Hofstede on Culture'. Hofstede Insights, n.d. https://geerthofstede.com/ (accessed 20 August 2021).

Hofstede, Geert, Gert Jan Hofstede, and Michael Minkov. *Cultures and Organizations: Software of the Mind*. Rev. and expanded 3rd ed. New York: McGraw-Hill USA, 2010.

Hofstede Insights. 'Compare Countries'. N.d. https://www.hofstedeinsights.com/product/compare-countries/ (accessed 20 August 2021).

Hofstede Insights. 'National Culture'. N.d. https://hi.hofstede-insights.com/national-culture (accessed 20 August 2021).

Hokusai. *Curious Japanese Watching Dutchmen on Dejima*, 1802. Rijksmuseum voor Volkenkunde, Leiden. https://commons.wikimedia.org/wiki/File:Curious_Japanese_watching_Dutchmen_on_Dejima.jpg.

Holmes, Thom. *Electronic and Experimental Music: Technology, Music, and Culture*. Oxfordshire: Routledge, 2012.

Holzer, Brigitte, Arthur Vreede and Gabriele Weigt. 'Introduction'. In *Disability in Different Cultures: Reflections on Local Concepts*, edited by Brigitte Holzer, Arthur Vreede and Gabriele Weigt, 9-23. Berlin: De Gruyter, 1999.

hooks, bell. 'Beyoncé's *Lemonade* is Capitalist Money-Making at Its Best'. *Guardian*, 11 May 2016. https://www.theguardian.com/music/2016/may/11/capitalism-of-beyonce-lemonade-album.

Horkheimer, Max, and Theodor W. Adorno. 'The Culture Industry: Enlightenment as Mass Deception'. In *Dialectic of Enlightenment*. Edited by Max Horkheimer et al., 94-136. Redwood City: Stanford University Press, 2020.

Huizinga, Johan. *Homo Ludens: A Study of the Play-Element in Culture*. Kettering: Angelico Press, 2016.

Huntington, Samuel. 'The Clash of Civilizations?' *Foreign Affairs* 72, no. 3 (1993): 22-49.

Hutter, Michael, and Bruno S. Frey. 'On the Influence of Cultural Value on Economic Value'. *Revue d'économie politique* 120 (2010): 35-46.

International Court of Justice. 'Separate Opinion of Vice-President Weeramantry'. 25 September 1997. https://www.icj-cij.org/public/files/case-related/92/092-19970925-JUD-01-03-EN.pdf.

International Court of Justice. 'Statute of the International Court of Justice'. N.d. https://www.icj-cij.org/en/statute.

International Criminal Court. 'About the Court'. https://www.icc-cpi.int/about (accessed 5 August 2021).

Jalabert, Charles. *Oedipus and Antigone*, 1842, oil on canvas, 45.2 in x 57.8 in. Musée des Beaux Arts, Marseilles. https://commons.wikimedia.org/wiki/File:The_Plague_of_Thebes.jpg.

Jara, Victor. 'El derecho de vivir en paz'. First released in 1971. Track 1 on *El derecho de vivir en paz*, Odeon Records, 1971.

Javaheri, Alireza. *Zoroastar Cube*. Panoramio, n.d., photograph. https://web.archive.org/web/20161031140814/http://www.panoramio.com/photo/117039973.

Jensen, Sune Qvotrup. 'Othering, Identity Formation and Agency'. *Qualitative Studies* 2, no. 2 (2001): 63-78. https://doi.org/10.7146/qs.v2i2.5510.

Johnson, Barbara. 'Anthropomorphism in Lyric and Law'. *Yale Journal of Law and the Humanities* 10, no. 2 (1998). https://digitalcommons.law.yale.edu/yjlh/vol10/iss2/15.

Josiehen. *Ravi Shankar with Anoushka Shankar at the World Sacred Music Festival in Fes, Morocco, in June 2005*. Wikimedia Commons, 4 June 2005, photograph. https://commons.wikimedia.org/wiki/File:Ravi_Shankar,_Fes_Sacred_Music_Festival.jpg.

Khachaturian, Aram. *Spartacus*. Choreography by Leonid Yakobson. Saint Petersburg. First staged on 27 December 1956.

King, Homay. 'Lost in Translation'. *Film Quarterly* 59, no. 1 (2005): 45-48. https://doi.org/10.1525/fq.2005.59.1.45.

Kishik, David. *Wittgenstein's Form of Life*. London: Continuum, 2008.

Korsten, Frans-Willem, and Tessa de Zeeuw, 'Towards a New Judicial Scene for Humans and Animals: Two Modes of Hypocrisy'. *Law and Literature* 27, no. 1 (2015): 23-47

Kossakovsky, Viktor, dir. SVYATO. Russia: Kossakovsky Film Production, 2005, film, 45 min., DVD.

Krog, Antjie, Nosisi Mpolweni, and Kopano Ratele. *There Was This Goat: Investigating the Truth Commission Testimony of Notrose Nobomvu Konile*. Scottsville, South Africa: University of KwaZulu-Natal Press, 2009.

Late Night Tales. *Deodato – Also sprach Zarathustra* [*2001*] (*Late Night Tales: At The Movies*). YouTube, 28 June 2011, video, 3:09. https://www.youtube.com/ watch?v=lGjGo-Aeot8.

Larousse dictionnaire de français. 'civilisation n.f.'. https://www.larousse.fr/diction-naires/francais/civilisation/16275 (accessed August 2021).

Leerssen, Joep. 'Nationalism and the Cultivation of Culture'. *Nations and Nationalism* 12, no. 4 (2006): 559-578.

Lefebvre, Henri. *State, Space, World: Selected Essays*. Minneapolis: University of Minnesota Press, 2009.

—. *The Urban Revolution*. Minneapolis: University of Minnesota Press, 2003.

—. *Writings on Cities*. Translated by Eleonore Kofman and Elizabeth Libas. Oxford: Blackwell, 1996.

Ligeti, György Ligeti. *Atmosphères: For Orchestra*. 1961.

Lloyd, Genevieve. *Routledge Philosophy Guidebook to Spinoza and* The Ethics. London: Routledge, 2002.

Low, Philip. 'The Cambridge Declaration of Consciousness'. Proclaimed at the Francis Crick Memorial Conference on Consciousness in Human and Non-Human Animals, Churchill College, University of Cambridge, 7 July 2012. https:// fcmconference.org/img/CambridgeDeclarationOnConsciousness.pdf.

Majumder, Auritro. 'Gayatri Spivak, Planetarity and the Labor of Imagining Internationalism'. *Mediations* 30, no. 2 (2017): 15-28. www.mediationsjournal. org/articles/planetarity.

Marino, Ori. 'Thinking Chickens: A Review of Cognition, Emotion, and Behavior in the Domestic Chicken'. *Animal Cognition*; 20, no. 2 (2017): 127-147.

Marotta, Vince. 'Zygmunt Bauman: Order, Strangerhood and Freedom'. *Thesis Eleven* 70, no. 2 (2002): 36-54.

Marx, Karl. *Economic and Philosophical Manuscripts: Early Writings*. Translated by Rodney Livingstone and Gregory Benton. London: Penguin Classics, 1992.

Mbembe, Achille. 'Necropolitics'. Translated by Libby Meintjes. *Public Culture* 15, no. 1 (2003): 11-40.

McFarland, Joel. 'Trends in Graduate Student Loan Debt'. NCES Blog, National Center for Education Statistics, 2 August 2018. https://nces.ed.gov/blogs/nces/ post/trendsin-graduate-student-loan-debt.

McKay, George. '"Crippled with Nerves": Popular Music and Polio, with Particular Reference to Ian Dury'. *Popular Music* 28, no. 3 (2009): 341-365. http://dx.doi. org/10.1017/S0261143009990109.

McLuhan, Marshall. *Understanding Media: The Extensions of Man*. London: Routledge, 2001.

Medunjanin, Amira. 'Jutros Mi Je Ruza Procvjetala'. First released in 2004. Track 2 on *Rosa*, Snail Records, 2004, CD.

Mehrotra, Nilika. 'Disability Rights Movements in India: Politics and Practice'. *Economic and Political Weekly* 46, no. 6 (2011), 65-72.

Merrifield, Andy. *Henri Lefebvre: A Critical Introduction*. New York: Routledge, 2006.

Mitcham, Carl. 'Philosophy and the History of Technology'. In *The History and Philosophy of Technology,* edited by George Bugliarello and Dean B. Donner. 163-198. Urbana: University of Illinois Press, 1979.

Mol, Annemarie. *Eating in Theory*. Durham, NC: Duke University Press, 2021.

Molina, Adrian, and Germaine Franco. 'The World Es Mi Familia'. First released on 10 November 2017. Track 6 on *Coco*. Walt Disney Music Company and Pixar Talking Pictures, 2017, CD.

Mouffe, Chantal. *On the Political*. London: Taylor and Francis, 2005.

Mozart, Wolfgang Amadeus. 'Mass in C Major ("Sparrow Mass"), K. 220/196b. Salzburg, 1775-1776.

Musicians without Borders. *Roses for Srebrenica*. YouTube, 14 July 2010, video, 5:11. https://www.youtube.com/watch?v=dFsIq7texk8.

Narasimhan, Subasri, and Paul P. Chandanabhumma. 'A Scoping Review of De-colonization in Indigenous-Focused Health Education and Behavior Research'. *Health Education & Behavior*, 3 June 2021. 10.1177/10901981211010095.

Nielsen, Kim E. *A Disability History of the United States*. Boston: Beacon Press, 2012.

—. 'Indigenous Peoples Day: Disability History and North American Indigenous Culture'. *Beacon Broadside*, 8 October 2012. Interview. https://www.beacon-broadside.com/broadside/2012/10/indigenous_peoples_day.html.

NPR. 'Ravi Shankar: Remembering A Master of the Sitar'. National Public Radio, 13 December 2012. https://www.npr.org/2012/12/14/167193821/ravi-shankar-remembering-a-master-of-thesitar?t=1628250035945.

Oxford English Dictionary. 3rd ed. Oxford: Oxford University Press, 2008.

Pessireron, Sylvia. *De verzwegen soldaat*. Antwerpen: The House of Books, 2012.

—. *Gesloten koffers*. Antwerpen: The House of Books, 2014.

—. *Molukkers in Nederland: Wij kwamen hier op dienstbevel*. Zwolle: Waanders, 2003.

—. *Trouwen in zeven 'Nederlandse' culturen*. Utrecht: Seram Press, 1998.

—. *Tussen mensen en geesten: Volksverhalen uit de Molukken*. Periplus, 1996.

Polak, Sara. *FDR in American Memory: Roosevelt and the Making of an Icon*. Baltimore, MD: Johns Hopkins University Press, 2021.

Putnam, Robert D. *Bowling Alone: The Collapse and Revival of American Community*. New York: Simon & Schuster, 2000.

Queen. 'The Show Must Go On'. First released on 14 October 1991. Track 12 on *Innuendo*. Parlophone Records Limited, 1991, CD.

Rand, Ayn, and Nathaniel Branden. *The Virtue of Selfishness: A New Concept of Egoism*. New York: Signet, 2014.

Rapaille, Clotaire. *The Culture Code.* New York: Broadway Books, 2006.

Redbone. 'We Were All Wounded at Wounded Knee'. First released on 13 September 1972. Track 10 on *Already Here (Expanded Edition).* Legacy Recordings, 1973, CD.

Rembrandt. *The Conspiracy of the Batavians under Claudius Civilis,* 1661-1662, oil on canvas, 196 cm x 309 cm, Nationalmuseum Stockholm. https://commons. wikimedia.org/wiki/File:Batavernastrohetsed.jpg.

Ross, Alex. 'Ligeti 1993: Searching for Music's Outer Limits'. *New York Times,* 20 March 1993.

Roy, Arundhati. *The God of Small Things.* London: Harper Collins, 1997.

Ryder, Richard. *The Political Animal: The Conquest of Speciesism.* Jefferson, NC: McFarland & Co., 1998.

Scheper-Hughes, Nancy, and Carolyn Sargent. *Small Wars: The Cultural Politics of Childhood.* Berkeley: University of California Press, 1999.

Scroll staff. 'Watch: A Soprano in Chile Defied the Silence Curfew to Sing "The Right to Live in Peace"'. *Scroll.in,* 4 November 2019. https://scroll.in/video/942523/watch-a-soprano-in-chile-defied-the-silence-curfew-to-sing-theright-to-live-in-peace (accessed August 2021).

Selasi, Taiye. 'Bye-bye Barbar'. *Callaloo* 36, no. 3 (2013): 528-530.

Shelley, Mary. *Frankenstein, or The Modern Prometheus.* Oxford: Oxford University Press, 2008.

Shohat Ella, and Robert Stam. *Unthinking Eurocentrism: Multiculturalism and the Media.* 2nd ed. London: Routledge, 2014.

Simard, Suzanne. *How Trees Talk to Each Other.* TED, June 2016, video, 18:10. https://www.ted.com/talks/suzanne_simard_how_trees_talk_to_each_other.

Simmel, Georg. 'The Stranger'. In *On Individuality and Social Forms,* 143-150. Chicago: University of Chicago Press, 1971.

Simon, Paul. 'Questions for the Angels'. First released on 12 April 2011. Track 8 on *So Beautiful or So What.* Hear Music, 2011.

Simondon, Gilbert. *Du mode d'existence des objets techniques.* 3rd ed. Paris: Aubier, 1989.

—. 'The Essence of Technicity'. Translated by Ninian Mellamphy, Dan Mellamphy and Nandita Biswas Mellamphy. *Deleuze Studies* 5 (2011): 406-424.

—. 'The Limits of Human Progress'. Translated by Sean Cubitt. *Cultural Politics* 8, no. 2 (2010): 229-236.

Simone, Nina. 'Ne me quitte pas'. First released in June 1965. Track 3 on *I Put a Spell on You.* Philips Records, 1965.

Soja, Edward W. *Seeking Spatial Justice.* Minneapolis: University of Minnesota Press, 2010.

Sommer, Iris. *De zeven zintuigen: Over waarnemen en onwaarnemen.* Amsterdam: Prometheus, 2018.

Spivak, Gayatri Chakravorty. 'Can the Subaltern Speak?' 'Can the subaltern speak? Speculations on widow-sacrifice' **Wedge** 7/8 (Winter/Spring): 120-130.

—. *Death of a Discipline*. New York: Columbia University Press, 2003.

—. *The Post-Colonial Critic: Interviews, Strategies, Dialogues*. Ed. Sarah Harasym. New York, Routledge, 1990.

—. 'The Rani of Sirmur: An Essay in Reading the Archives'. *History and Theory* 24, no. 3 (1985): 247-272.

Stanley, David. *A Gamelan Orchestra Playing at a Cremation Ceremony on Kuta Beach, Bali*. Wikimedia Commons, 12 November 2011, photograph. https://en.m.wikipedia.org/wiki/File:Gamelan_Orchestra_(6336847793).jpg.

Swedberg, Richard. 'A Note on Civilizations and Economies'. *European Journal of Social Theory* 13, no. 1 (2010): 15-30.

Tagore, Rabindranath. 'India's National Anthem'. First publicly recited 27 December 1911.

Tambling, Jeremy. 'Prologue: City-Theory and Writing, in Paris and Chicago: Space, Gender, Ethnicity'. *The Palgrave Handbook of Literature and the City*, edited by Jeremy Tambling, 1-22. London: Palgrave/Macmillan, 2016.

Taylor, Charles. *Sources of the Self: The Making of Modern Identity*. Cambridge, MA: Harvard University Press, 1989.

Tonkiss, Fran. 'The Ethics of Indifference'. *International Journal of Cultural Studies* 6, no. 3 (2003): 297-311. https://doi.org/10.1177/13678779030063004.

Tönnies, Ferdinand. *Community and Association*. Translated by Charles P. Loomis. London: Routledge and Kegan Paul, 1955.

—. *Community and Civil Society*. Edited by Jose Harris and translated by Jose Harris and Margaret Hollis. Cambridge: Cambridge University Press, 2001.

—. *Gemeinschaft und Gesellschaft: Grundbegriffe der Reinen Soziologie*. Darmstadt: Wissenschaftliche Buchgesellschaft, 1991.

Trajectina, Camerata. 'Hoe die Spaanse hoeren komen klagen'. Track 3 on *Wilhelmus en de anderen*. Amsterdam University Press, 2015, CD.

Truth and Reconciliation Committee. 'Human Rights Violations: Hearings & Submissions'. Commission website, n.d. https://www.justice.gov.za/trc/hrvtrans/index.htm.

Tweedy, Ann C. 'From Beads to Bounty: How Wampum Became America's First Currency – and Lost Its Power'. *Indian Country Today*, 5 October 2017. https://indiancountrytoday.com/archive/from-beads-to-bounty-how-wampum-became-americas-first-currencyand-lost-its-power.

Typhoon. 'We zijn er'. First released in 2014. Track 1 on *Lobi Da Basi*. Top Notch Records, 2014, CD.

Typhoon [@mctyphoon]. 'Net staande gehouden door de politie in Zwolle'. *Instagram*, 30 May 2016. https://www.instagram.com/p/BGCaWb6vkOc/?utm_source=ig_embed.

Uexküll, Jakob Johann von. *A Foray into the Worlds of Animals and Humans with a Theory of Meaning.* Minneapolis: University of Minnesota Press, 2010.

UNESCO. 'Protecting Our Heritage and Fostering Creativity'. United Nations Educational, Scientific and Cultural Organization, n.d. https://en.unesco.org/themes/protecting-our-heritage-and-fostering-creativity (accessed 3 August 2021).

Values Project, The. 'What Are Australian Values?' 16 August 2018. https://www.thevaluesproject.com/blog/what-are-australian-values/.

Van Ertvelde, Anaïs, and Andries Hiskes. 'Disability and Academia: A Strange Pair?' Leideninclusionblog (Leiden University), 29 October 2020. https://leideninclusionblog.nl/articles/disability-and-academia-a-strange-pair.

Verlag J.J. Weber. *Barrikade während des Spartakusaufstandes/Barricade during the Spartacus Uprising.* Wikimedia Commons, 15 August 2015, photograph. https://commons.wikimedia.org/wiki/File:Spartakusaufstand_Barrikaden.jpg.

Vertovec, Steven. 'Super-diversity and Its Implications'. *Ethnic and Racial Studies* 30, no. 6 (2007): 1024-1054. doi:10.1080/01419870701599465.

Vugts, Berrie. 'The Case against Animal Rights: A Literary Intervention'. PhD diss., Leiden University, 2015.

Waldschmidt. Anne. 'Disability Goes Cultural: The Cultural Model of Disability as an Analytical Tool'. In *Culture-Theory-Disability: Encounters between Disability Studies and Cultural Studies*, 19-28. Bielefeld: Transcript Verlag, 2017.

Walkowitz, Rebecca L. 'Translating the Untranslatable: An Interview with Barbara Cassin'. *Public Books*, 15 June 15 2014. https://www.publicbooks.org/translating-the-untranslatable-an-interview-with-barbara-cassin/.

Walzer, Michael. *Spheres of Justice: A Defense of Pluralism and Equality.* La Vergne: Ingram Publishers, 1984.

Web Exclusive, '"Cartoonist Lives Matter": Art Spiegelman Responds to Charlie Hebdo Attack, Power of Cartoons' *Democracy Now* 8 January 2015. https://www.democracynow.org/2015/1/8/cartoonists_lives_matter_art_spiegelman_responds

Wendell, Susan. *The Rejected Body: Feminist Philosophical Reflections on Disability.* Oxfordshire: Taylor and Francis, 1996.

Wheeler, Lorna. '"Shave 'em Dry": Lucille Bogan's Queer Blues'. In *Transgression and Taboo: Critical Essays*, edited by Nandita Batra and Vartan P. Messier, 161-187. Mayagüez, Puerto Rico: College English Association: Caribbean Chapter Publications, 2005.

Wild Ambience. 'Australian Magpie: Song & Calls'. https://wildambience.com/wildlife-sounds/australian-magpie/ (accessed 22 November 2021).

Winehouse, Amy. 'Tears Dry on Their Own'. First released on 13 August 2007. Track 7 on *Back to Black*. Island Records, 2006, CD.

Whitman, Walt. 'By Blue Ontario's Shore'. The Walt Whitman Archive. https://whitmanarchive.org/published/LG/1881/poems/197.

Wikipedia. 'Value (economics)'. https://en.wikipedia.org/wiki/Value_(economics) (accessed 7 August 2021).

Wohlleben, Peter. *The Hidden Life of Trees: What They Feel, How They Communicate – Discoveries from a Secret World.* Translated by Jane Billinghurst. Vancouver: Greystone Books, 2016.

Working Gringos, The. 'Commercial Octopus Farming in Sisal'. *Yuktan Living*, 3 May 2010. https://yucatanliving.com/posts/commercial-octopus-farming-in-sisal/.

WWF-Canada. *Humpback Whale Singing in the Great Bear Sea.* YouTube, 14 December 2012, video, 3:17. https://www.youtube.com/watch?v=JSgrFH11aiI.

X, Malcolm. '(1964) Malcolm X's Speech at the Founding Rally of the Organization of Afro-American Unity'. BlackPast, 16 October 2007. https://www.blackpast.org/african-american-history/speeches-african-americanhistory/1964-malcolm-x-s-speech-founding-rally-organization-afro-american-unity/

Yindi, Yothu. 'Tribal Voice'. Lyrics by Mandawuy. First released in September 1991. Track 3 on *Tribal Voice*. Mushroom Records, 1991.

Žižek, Slavoj. *Tarrying with the Negative: Kant, Hegel and the Critique of Ideology.* Durham, NC: Duke University Press, 1993.

Index of terms

Index of names